THE SOUL OF INDIA

THE SOUL OF INDIA

A
CONSTRUCTIVE STUDY
OF
INDIAN THOUGHTS & IDEALS

BY
BIPIN CHANDRA PAL

GYAN

Published by

Gyan Publishing House
5, Ansari Road
Daryaganj, New Delhi-110002
Phone: 011-47034999, 9811692060
E-mail: books@gyanbooks.com

Distribution Network
gyanbooks.com
India, USA, Canada, UK, Australia, France

ISBN: 978-81-212-8236-9 (PB)
First Published, 1911

2nd Impression 2023

Printed at: Gyan Press, Delhi.

THE SOUL OF INDIA
Author: BIPIN CHANDRA PAL

THE SOUL OF INDIA

A

CONSTRUCTIVE STUDY

OF

INDIAN THOUGHTS & IDEALS

BY

BIPIN CHANDRA PAL

Published by

CHOUDHURY & CHOUDHURY

CALCUTTA:

1911.

Bipin Chandra Pal

Publishers' Preface.

Babu Bipin Chandra Pal needs no introduction to his fellow-countrymen in India. But we feel as if a few words of introduction might be welcome by the foreign readers for whom the present volume is specially intended. And the publishers can do no better to meet this need, than reproduce here a very appreciative Character Sketch of Mr. Pal by Mr. W. T. Stead that appeared in the last October number of his Review of Reviews. This Sketch will give the European reader some idea of the Author, who, as the Modern Review, the premier English Monthly of India, once said, " has, of all Indian politicians

a most thorough grasp of Indian sociology and civilisation."

Mr. BIPIN CHANDRA PAL:

NATIONALIST-IMPERIALIST.

After spending three years in this country in a condition of almost enforced exile Mr. Bipin Chandra Pal has returned to India. He sailed for Bombay on the 20th of last month. Mr. Pal, who, formerly editor of *New India*, was one of the leaders of the Indian National movement, was also closely connected with the attempt to foster the national spirit by boycotting foreign goods. His patriotism, although much appreciated by his fellow-countrymen, was not regarded in the same light by the Government, and Mr. Pal, like many a better man, had to spend a certain period of his novitiate in gaol. Shortly after his release he left India and came to this country, where he has been pretty constantly in evidence as a speaker on Indian topics, particularly those connected with Hindu philosophy.

A PERSONAL TRIBUTE.

I have had the pleasure of Mr. Chandra Pal's acquaintance since his arrival in this country, and I feel sincere regret at his departure. None of the Indian Nationalists who have come to this country of late years have left quite such a good impression upon my mind, for Mr. Pal, while never abating in the least the fervour of his Nationalist aspirations, has a width of outlook and a well-balanced impartial judgment which is rare to find in any man, let alone in a Nationalist who has suffered imprisonment for his cause. I have heard Mr. Pal lecture, and I have met him frequently at my own house, where he has ever been an honoured and a welcome guest. Now he has left England there is no one who can exactly fill his place.

HIS ACTIVITY IN BRITAIN.

Mr. Chandra Pal has lectured a good deal for the Ethical Society, especially in London and the provinces. He has also taken an active interest in the propaganda of the Labour and Radical Parties. As a speaker he is fluent ; his voice is good and resonant, and he is very quick at what the Scotch call the "up-tak'." As a lecturer and political speaker he has been very popular, and his gift of exposition is such that even his lectures upon Hindu philosophy have succeeded in holding audiences among whom philosophy of any kind was not exactly a daily study. Mr. Chandra Pal, so far from having any reason to complain of lack of sympathy on the part of the common people of this country, takes back with him to India grateful reminiscences of unfailing hospitality and a courteous anxiety to hear the Nationalists' point of view from a Nationalist leader. He has, of course, been thrown mostly among Labour men. Socialists, Home Rulers, and more or less advanced thinkers of our people, and this may account for the fact that never once during his sojourn amongst us has he experienced the slightest discourtesy, nor has he been conscious of suffering any disability on account of his nationality or his colour.

HIS WORK AMONG INDIAN STUDENTS.

I asked Mr. Pal on the eve of his departure what had been the chief object of his teachings in England ; what had he tried to teach us ?

He said his work had been laid quite as much among his own countrymen as among mine. In fact, he seemed disposed to regard his work among the Indian youths who are studying in England as of more importance than his effort to expound the Indian Nationalist ideal to the English people.

* * * * *

INDIA MUST DEVELOP ALONG HER OWN LINES.

"I have also endeavoured always to teach both to the English and to the Hindus that India's future must be a matter of national development. We do not wish Parliamentary or any other institutions to be imposed upon us from without ; we wish to evolve our own institutions in harmony with our national history and our national characteristics. I have been much misunderstood by those who are clamouring for Colonial self-government in India, as in Canada or Australia. The fundamental bases upon which self-government rests in these Dominions are not to be found in India. In the self-governing Dominions the population is for the most part of British stock, allied to you in race, religion, literature and traditions. They are bone of your bone and flesh of your flesh. To assume that institutions which can safely be granted to such people can also be conceded to races which have nothing, either ethically or ethnically, in common with you is preposterous We have to recognise facts as they are, and to realise that in a political controversy it is well to be honest and frank, and not to veil a demand for one thing under the pretence of wanting a very different thing.

WANTED--A SPIRITUAL REVIVAL.

"What I want in India," said Mr. Chandra Pal, "is the growth of a great spiritual revival among the people. This has already begun. India's power lies in the realm of thought rather than in the realm of matter. The more our people can be infused and enthused with the ideas of the great teachers who have moulded the thought and life of successive generations of Indian people, the more potent will be their influence on outside nations, the more close their internal union in spiritual brotherhood. So far the Indian national movement has not any vitality or any hope of success ; that secret must be sought in the fact that it is a religious revival, a revival free from fanaticism, but rich in its promise of political as well as of spiritual benefit to our people."

I said to Mr. Pal, "If that is what you have tried to teach us, what have we succeeded in teaching you?"

WHAT HE HAS LEARNED HERE.

"I will be quite frank with you," said Mr. Pal. "I have learned a great deal in the three years, but one thing more than all else stands out before my mind. I am more deeply impressed than ever I was with the immense influence which might be wielded in the future of the history of the world by Britain and India acting together. Such co-operation mnst be, of course, based upon a recognition of the right of India to be treated as a free and equal partner and not as a free dependent in the Empire. Let us suppose that the British Government in India were to be reconstituted on a basis which would give the freest possible scope of self-fulfilment to India, and yet continue the Association known now as the British Empire. It would be a federal constitution, the freedom of the federated parts being realised in and through the unity of the federal whole. Such a partnership between Great Britain and India, speaking as a man who has the broadest interests of humanity at heart, would be preferable to an isolated independence for India.

BRITAIN'S NEED OF INDIA.

"If, for instance, the Almighty were to offer me in one hand an isolated independent India, a sovereign State entirely free from all connection with other States, and in the other hand were to offer an India united with Great Britain and her Colonies and Egypt in terms of loyal partnership based on freedom and justice, I would unhesitatingly choose the latter rather than the former. I have been led to this by reflecting upon the great problems which threaten to convulse the world in the near future. These problems are three in number. There is, first, the problem of the white against the coloured races. All over the world the white races seem to be coming together, shoulder to shoulder, preparing for an inevitable conflict with the more numerous, but at present politically dependent, people with coloured skins. The second question is that of Pan-Islamism. You are inclined to belittle the significance of a Mahomedan revival. I tell you that you are making a mistake. There is latent in Islam the capacity for great spiritual intentification, which may flame out all over the world in a way which may confound all your politics. The third question is that of the Mongolian confederacy. One-fourth of the human race lies in the Chinese reservoir, inert, motionless at present ; but there is a stirring in the placid waters, and who can tell what will result if the Chinese should emerge from their age-long seclusion and compete with the other races for the commerce and control of the world ?

THE HOPE OF THE FUTURE.

" These three problems are among the unsettled questions which have no mercy for the peace of nations. Yet in all three it seems to me that Britain and India united will be able to exercise a far more potent influence for the avoidance of war and the arrangement of some *modus vivendi* than could be done either by Britain alone or by India alone. It is in the combination of Britain and India that my hope of the future lies. I object to call it an Empire. I would rather call it a co-operative partnership. Such a co-operative partnership between Great Britain and India would enable the partners to interpose with unequalled authority as peace-makers whenever there threatened to come a clash between the white and coloured races. From the wealth of their experience they could afford examples to the others as to the composing of differences and the removal of prejudice. So it is in relation to the Pan-Islamic danger. The backbone of Pan-Islamism lies in India. A dim consciousness of the importance of the Mahomedan element is penetrating even now the minds of our rulers, but a contented and self-governing India and Egypt on co-operative lines with great Britain would remove the Pan-Islamic menace, if not entirely, at least more effectively than by any other means that mankind has yet conceived.

"Upon the teeming millions of Chinese the influence of the British-Indian co-partnership would be exercised chiefly from the spiritual influence of India, but that is a more remote question. The clash between the white and coloured races and the danger of Pan-Islamism are immediately pressing dangers, and to cope with them both no instrument could be calculated to produce such good results as a co-operative union between Britain and India."

A CO-OPERATIVE PARTNERSHIP.

"What would you say were the conditions of such a co-operative partnership ?" I said.

"Absolute equality and justice," said he. "India would not be sacrificed to Britain nor Britain sacrificed to India."

"But how would that work out in relation to the Colonies, who certainly do not treat their Indian fellow-subjects with either equality or justice ?"

"That is very simple," said Mr. Pal. "I recognise fully that it is impossible for you to compel the self-governing Dominions to treat their Indian fellow-subjects with equality and justice. But a self-governing India would do it easily. For what is there to hinder the Indian Government enforcing against all British subjects resident in the Dominions the same regulations, if they wish to come to India or trade with India, that they inflict upon Indian subjects who wish to go to South Africa or Australia ? We would prefer equality on a basis of equal rights, but if we cannot have equality on the basis of equal rights, let us have equality on the basis of equal wrongs. That is to say, let every South African or Australian who visits India be subjected to exactly the same indignities and disabilities that

South Africans and Australians deem it wise to inflict upon Indians. At present, while they inflict all manner of disabilities upon our people, the British Indian Government accords to them all the liberties which are enjoyed by the citizens of the United Kingdom, which rarely admits Indians to all the advantages of citizenship."

The idea is worth while thinking over, and I heartily commend these remarks of Mr. Chandra Pal, not only to his own countrymen in India, but especially to the Anglo-Indian rulers in that country and to the colonists, who at present imagine they can have everything their own way in dealing with the Indians. Mr. Pal's claim for equality in disabilities if they cannot have equality in privileges is undeniably just, and may some day be enforced in a fashion which may compel some high-flying gentlemen in our Dominions to reconsider their position. Apart from that, Mr. Pal's views as to the desirability, in the interest of humanity, of the close working partnership between Britain and India are well worthy of the consideration of the statesman and the philosopher, regardless of nationality.

Author's Apologia.

——:o:——

This book is very far indeed, from what it should have been.

To many people it will seem to lack that presentation of details without which it is not easy to understand the idealities underlying every culture and civilisation. No one can regret this deficiency more than I do.

If God grants me life and inspiration, I shall try to remove it in a subsequent volume, which will apply the generalisations presented here to the interpretation of the social and economic life and institutions of the country.

In presenting Sree Krishna as The Soul of India, I may be accused of sectarian prepossessions. But Krishna is not here presented as a sectarian

Ideal; but as the Principle and Personality in and through whom, as in the past so also in the present and even in the future, the great Indian Synthesis was, is being, and will be worked.

The Soul of Europe and America is Christ: the Soul of India is, in the same way, Sree Krishna.

The articles in Part II. appeared in the *Modern Review* above the name of E. Willis.

CONTENTS.

—:o:—

LETTER I.

Fundamental Considerations.

LETTER II.

The Name and The Thing.

LETTER III.

India : The Mother.

LETTER IV.

Religious India.

PART II.

Some World Problems.

The Problem of Civilisation.

The Problem of Nationality and Empire.

Bijoy Krishna Goswami

ओं

——इहा आमि किछुइ ना जानि,
य तुमि कहाओ सेइ कहि आमि वाणी ।
तोमार शिक्षाय पडि़ येन शुक पाँठ ,
साक्षात् ईश्वर तुमि, के बुझे तोमार नाट ?
हृदये प्रेरण कर, जिह्वाय कहाओ वाणी ,
कि कहिब भाल मन्द किछुइ ना जानि ॥

—चैतन्य महाप्रभु प्रति रामानन्द वाक्यम् ।
चै: च: मध्यलीला, ८म प:

OM

Nought, excepting this I know
That what from my lips doth flow
Is what thou bid'st me say.

And what I pour from out my throat
Parrot-like I learn by rote
From thee Lord! each day.

A present God thou art, and none
Can fathom what by thee is done
In sport or playful mood.

This heart with thoughts thou e'er dost fill
This tongue with speech providest still,
I know not ill or good.

ओं

श्री श्रीगुरवे नमः ।

THE SOUL OF INDIA.

LETTER I.

FUNDAMENTAL CONSIDERATIONS.

PERSONAL AND PREFATORY.

I AM sincerely thankful that you are not coming out to India this season. You will, perhaps, think it cruel of me to be so glad at what must have been a sore disappointment to you. But though I did not actually discourage you, I never really liked the idea of your coming to see us just yet. The time is not yet, my child, when you could profitably come face to face with our life and institutions. There is as yet a very large element of poetic fancy in your admiration for India. You have read something of our past history and achievements and have been profoundly impressed with the grandeur of our ancient civilisation. Indeed, it is a commonplace of present day European thought, to speak in high terms of our past. Even Mr. Theodore Roosevelt could not refuse to admit that we were highly civilised at one time, though that high and ancient civilisation has, somehow "gone crooked" in our day. This is the general European estimate of modern India. I know you strongly resented the flighty utterances of the ex-American President. But yet I am not sure whether even to you, direct and living contact with our present life and habits would not come as something of a rude shock. Few Europeans have had a greater love and regard for Indian thought and life than the late Prof. Max Muller. Yet even Max

Muller refused all through his life to come out to India, lest his idealism should be destroyed by our present day actualities. Max Muller's appreciation was essentially intellectual. Yours, I know, is much deeper; it is spiritual. It is the special privilege of your sex to seize the spiritual where we, mere men, even at our best, can rarely go beyond the intellectual. But still even you require a further period of aloofness and training to be able to truly enter into the inner spirit of our complex life and culture. This is why I am so glad that you are not coming out to India so soon. Cherish your virgin romance religiously. Seek not, my child, to lift the veil off the face of this Beautiful Mystery before the due term of your novitiate is over. I want you to come to us not as a tourist, nor as a mere student, but as a pilgrim, in love and reverence; for it is only then that you will be able to know what India is today, what she was in the past, and what, in the Providence of God, she must be in the near future, to be able to fulfil her divinely-ordained mission to that Universal Humanity towards which, consciously or unconsciously, the nations of the world are moving so fast in our time.

ENGLISH WORKS ON INDIA.

You want to know what books I would recommend to you to help you in your further study and understanding of our life and thought. Truth to say, there is not one that I know of which I would wish you to read now. There is no dearth of English books on India. They are the works of Anglo-Indian officials and European tourists. Every publishing season in London and New York is adding to their number. I can not say that I have read them all. But in a general way I am fairly acquainted with the character of these books, and I may say without offence, that none of these reveal the real soul of India. Their authors are not to blame for it. Most of them have done their best. And it is not their fault that they had not the right key for opening our door.

These books may be broadly divided into three classes. The first deal largely with ancient India. They are written by European Orientalists. Max Muller and Monier Williams, Macdonald and Rhys Davis and others in our day; Sir William Jones, Horace Hayman Wilson, and Muir and others in the early eighteenth century, have given to the English-speaking world the result of their lifelong studies in ancient Sanskrit literature or Indo-Aryan civilisation. Christian Missionaries from the days of Carey, Marshman, and Ward, have tried frequently to discuss the religious life and institutions of our land. Anglo-Indian officials have also placed on record, now and again, their impressions and memories of the country where they spent the greater part of their active life. But I know not of one single book among all these that has seized the full truth and reality of our life and culture. The best of these are like Max Muller's "India What It Can Teach Us," the worst, I think, are like Sir J. D. Rees's "Real India."

THE INTERPRETATION OF INDIA BY ORIENTALISTS.

Max Muller and other Orientalists know something, no doubt, of our past, and speak in terms almost of exaggerated admiration of that past. But almost invariably they leave the sad impression upon the reader's mind that all that they say are mere matters of ancient history, have an academic and antiquarian interest only, but no reference to the actualities of the present; and that though India was, undoubtedly, highly civilised at a time when the puissant nations of the modern world had scarcely emerged out of primitive barbarism, the India of to-day is not only different from the India of the Vedas, the Upanishads or the great Epics, but has irretrievably fallen away from that high position. Max Muller was so keenly conscious of this pitiful disparity between ancient and modern India, that he persistently refused, as I have said, to come to this country, lest his dream-picture of our land and people should be cruelly destroyed. The fact of the matter really is that neither Max Muller nor any other European Orientalist has been able to seize the true course of historic evolution in India. Not one of them, so far as I know, has been able to grasp the truth that age after age, and epoch after epoch there have been evolution and progress in India as elsewhere, that this process of progressive evolution was never stopped at any period of our history and it is going on as much to-day as it did at the time of the Vedas, the Upanishads, or the Epics. And their failure to recognise this elementary fact has vitiated all their judgment of Indian life and civilisation.

MISSIONARY PRESENTATIONS.

As regards the works of European Christian Missionaries, these are generally of a contentious character, written with the natural prepossessions of the religious propagandist, and are, consequently, without any value as a correct exposition of our religious ideals and institutions. They have naturally applied the canons of Christianity to the interpretation of an apparently different order of religious experience and symbolism. There is, no doubt, a very close affinity between the deeper strains of Christian and Hindu thought. There is a high level of spiritual life and thought, where both the advanced Christian and the advanced Hindu, particularly of the Vaishnavic or Shaivite Schools,—the Schools of Love and Faith in Hinduism—speak of the same eternal truths, though in different language and through their own peculiar symbols. Unfortunately, however, Christian propagandism in India, as, in fact, in every non-Christian land, has but little appreciation of these deeper affinities. The outer shells, the external symbols and the popular dogmas and rituals of these two great world-religions are what the ordinary, unillumined, and unspiritual votaries of either recognise and know in the other. Naturally therefore, the carnal conflcts of ununderstood dogmas and lifeless symbols, have almost invariably vitiated the judgment of the ordinary, unspiritual Hindu, of the truth and reality of Christianity and that of the ordinary Christian propagandist of the truth and reality of Hinduism. Missionary presentations of Indian life and religion are not only unreliable, but are often even needlessly offensive to Indian susceptibilities.

WORKS BY ANGLO-INDIAN OFFICIALS.

The third class of books, written by Anglo-Indian officials, generally deal with the particularities of official life and experience, and discuss present-day economic, social and administrative problems. The British officials in India, like the Christian Missionaries, have also the peculiar prejudices and prepossessions of their own class and country. They are the children of modern Europe, steeped in the spirit of what is called modern civilisation, and even the ablest of them cannot help applying, in their study and judgment of Indian life and institutions, the generalisations of European history and culture. They have little or no consciousness of the fact that Indian experience belongs to a somewhat different order from that of Europe, and the generalisations of the one cannot be reasonably applied to the interpretation of the other. Besides, the India which British officials know most intimately is that which the introduction of English education and the superimposition of British institutions, both economic and political, upon an ancient and civilized people, have created.

They come face to face only with that side of our life and character which is open to official contact and alien influences. Behind and beyond this, there is our larger social and domestic life, and our still more large and deep religious and spiritual life. Of this the Anglo-Indian officials know little and understand even less. It is quite natural, therefore, that they too, inspite of their long residence in the country and their intimate official connections with the people they rule, have failed as much as the others, to enter into the inner spirit of our life and culture.

MISLEADING NOT DISHONEST.

But however imperfect and misleading their presentation of Indian life and culture may be, I do not by any means say or suggest that even the most incompetent of these European writers on India have been guilty of deliberate misrepresentation. They have tried to faithfully record what they have actually seen or heard. But they usually forget the common truth that what we see or hear are mere externals and appearances.

Sense-testimony is no doubt absolute on the physical plane. When, therefore, the European scientist studies the physical features of our land, when he mensurates our fields, trigonometrates our altitudes and undulations, investigates our animal, or our vegetable, or our mineral kingdoms, the records of his study and investigations are accepted as true and authoritative. But the study of man belongs altogether to a different plane. The specific organs of truth in the domain of the psychological, the sociological, and the spiritual sciences are not our senses. Here also the eye sees, the ear hears; but the real meaning of what is seen or heard is supplied not by the senses, but by the understanding, which interprets what is seen or heard in the light of its own peculiar experiences and associations.

AN ANCIENT HINDU INTERPRETATION OF THE EUCHARIST.

Ages ago, in the very infancy of the Christian era, a Hindu traveller went on a visit to some Christian Colony, probably in Asia Minor. The story of this visit has been described in the NARADIYA UPAKHYANA, of the Sanskrit Epic, Mahabharata. We read here that the author of this Upakhyana came accross a peculiar religious sect who "ate up the God they worshipped.' Seen with the eye alone, it is a faithful description of the Christian sacrament of the Eucharist or the Holy Communion. The priest blesses the bread and wine placed on the communion table. He mutters some prayers over these. He does so in an attitude of worship. To those who are used to the worship of the Deity through symbols or images, the communion service would naturally appear as a worship of bread and wine. And when the consecrated bread and wine are distributed among the congregation, they do appear to be "eating the God they worshipped." The writer saw from the outside; cognised with his senses certain physical acts of the Christian worshippers. He had not the right key to the interpretation of these outer acts. He put his own meaning on these in the light of his own peculiar experience. What he saw was a fact, yet how misleading is his interpretation of what he had seen! And the story illustrates very clearly, the general character of the interpretations put upon our life and institutions by European scholars and students.

AN EUROPEAN INTERPRETATION OF OUR "NAKEDNESS."

A few months ago an eminent British journalist came out to India, to study the present situation in the country. The very first thing that he communicated to the journal he represented was the disgusting nakedness of our populations. Such nakedness is almost entirely unknown in Europe or

America. Lack of decent clothing is associated there with squalid poverty, dirt and drink,—the result of intellectual inferiority or moral deterioration. People there have also read of the naked cannibal, in books of travel. The seminudity of our teeming populations is, therefore, naturally interpreted, by the superficial European observer, as a proof of our semibarbarism. He forgets, however, that peoples' dress, like the wool of animals, is determined, in the natural course of their evolution, almost entirely by the climatic character of their habitat. Our short and thin loin-cloths and bare upper limbs are almost a stern necessity in our sweating, sweltry climate. Nature demands this of us. They are no more a proof of our barbarism than is the opera or ball dress of fashionable Western society, which cannot even plead such natural necessity, any proof of the lower culture or character of Europe. As with our national dress, so also with all our social or domestic institutions. They have had a long course of historic evolution behind them. Whatever their present moral or physical value, whether they be good or they be bad in the judgment of the modern man,—they owe their origin and development to imperious historic needs, grew out of the natural attempt of our social organism to adapt itself, from epoch to epoch, to its changing environment, both physical and social. And this being the case, they can only be rightly understood and interpreted in the light of our general history and culture. Unfortunately, however, few European writers on India get the right perspective of our history and evolution. They come from the outside. They carry with them all the prepossessions and prejudices of their own country and culture. They observe the externals of our life and institutions. And even the best of them see India as a company of blind people, in the story cited in our logical text-books—"saw" the elephant.

AS THE BLIND "SAW" THE ELEPHANT.

The blind people of a village, so runs this old story, once went to see an elephant that had come to their neighbourhood. They were led near the animal, and standing around it, each man put out his hand to feel how it was like. One man stroked the trunk of the elephant, another its ear, a third its leg, a fourth its tail; and thus they "saw" the elephant. Coming home they commenced to describe the animal to their friends. The man who had stroked its trunk said that it was like a large python. He who had stroked its ear, contended that it was like an immense winnowing fan. He who had felt its leg swore that the elephant was like a huge pillar. What each of these blind men said was absolutely true so far as his own particular sense-knowledge went: yet how monstrously false it was as a picture of the elephant! Similarly what the European writers on India record is, in a sense, strictly true so far as their own particular sense-impressions go. Yet it may be,—indeed most frequently is—all the same, monstrously false, as a picture of Real India.

Some writers have seen only a particular Indian province, and have confidently presented the particularities of their limited and superficial experience, as a general statement of truth about Indian life and civilisation. Others, with a wider range of experience, have been impressed with the endless varieties of our provincial and ethnic life and institutions, but have absolutely failed to seize the fundamental unity that stands behind these bewildering diversities. They have all seen India as the blind people in the story "saw" the elephant.

AS THE FISHES KNEW THE SEA.

An Anglo-Indian official once declared that he had spent thirty years of the best part of his life in India, and claimed, therefore, to speak with the authority of the specialist on Indian history and civilisation. But he forgot that mere physical contact with a thing does not necessarily lead to a full and correct knowledge of it.

The fishes of the sea, so runs a Chinese story, once went in a body to the big, wise fish, and wanted to know what the sea was like. Yet they had lived all their life in that self-same sea ! The story was evidently invented to drive home a fundamental theological truth, but may be repeated here to illustrate a very common Anglo-Indian error, in regard to Indian life and institutions.

THE RECORDER AND THE INTERPRETER.

The fact, really, is that even the oldest European residents in India can as a class, claim only what may be called a mere sense-contact with our life and habits. Except under very exceptional circumstances, even neither much learning nor close research can help them to a more intimate veiw of our character and culture. For our senses can never take us beyond the apparent and the objective. The function of the senses is simply to record outer impressions; but not to interpret them. Even on the physical plane, while the records of phenomena come from the senses, their intelligent interpretation, which alone raises these to the position of science, is always supplied by the mind. In fact the natural or the physical order with which our senses deal, is not absolutely sensuous either. Had it been so, our knowledge of physical phenomena would have belonged to the same class as that of the lower animals, would consist of isolated and unsystematised sense-impressions only. The physical sciences have been made possible upon the assumption that the outer and sensuous natural order does not stand by itself, but is co-related to our inner mental order, and, therefore, admits of being rightly interpreted in the terms of our thought or reason. But while there is a general agreement among men of equal intelligence and education, in regard to the interpretation of physical phenomena, there is no such agreement in regard to the interpretation of the more complex mental and spiritual experiences; and the standard of judgment in regard to human activities and institutions is, therefore, fundamentally different from that which is applied to the interpretation of physical facts. Here the standard is essentially psychological and spiritual, determined by the character of the intellectual and socio-ethical life and ideals of the observer, and it widely differs in different persons, owing to differences in their mental temperament and training.

ANOTHER HINDU STORY.

Three men, so goes another popular Hindu story, once simultaneously heard the exclamation—"Alas! the night is gone." One of them was a devotee, engaged in his early morning devotions; the second a lover, in the company of his love; and the third a burglar, prowling about for robbery. And these three men put three different interpretations upon this one, simple, exclamation! The devotee thought,—"Here is a holy man, repenting the loss of so many precious hours of the night in sleep, which should have been spent in meditation and prayer." The lover thought,—"Here is another unfortunate person like myself whom the signs of breaking dawn are threatening with cruel seperation from his love." The thief thought,—"lo! here is another poor beggar who have had, evidently, no chance to rob any body to-night." We are all, whether ignorant or wise, like these people, always putting our own meaning, in the light of ou special temperament or experience, upon men and things. The European does so in regard to things Indian; even the Indian, with much less excuse, in view of the peculiarly catholic, synthetic, and universal spirit of his race and culture,—is doing the same in regard to things European. More than half their mutual misunderstandings are due to this cause. They forget the fundamental difference, both of temperament and training, that exists between them.

THE DIFFERENCE BETWEEN THE EUROPEAN AND THE INDIAN.

This difference may, I think, be best explained by a reference to the peculiar constitutions of the Hindu and the Greek mind. For these two ancient peoples may well be taken as typical of the two great world-cultures, that India and Europe respectively represent. Indian culture is not absolutely Hindu, nor is the European culture absolutely Greek. Like all great world-cultures, they are both of a complex and composite character. Many races and many cultures have contributed to their growth and evolution. But still the main current of European culture has flowed from Greece, and the central stream of Indian culture has flowed through the Hindu people. These two world-cultures have received their special features, mainly, if not entirely, from these two great divisions of the Indo-Aryan race, respectively.

THE GREEK AND THE HINDU.

As members of the same race, there are, necessarily, many fundamental affinities between the Greek and the Hindu. Their physical structure is fundamentally the same. Generally speaking, the Hindu has the same regular features, the same straight or curly hair, the same shape of the cranium, as the Greek; and whatever variations are observed between them to-day, whether in cut or in colour, are entirely due to what the

Anthropologist calls miscegenation or mixture with other stocks. But all these differences notwithstanding, the original physical affinities beween these two peoples are too marked to be ignored. Like their original physical structure, the fundamental social structure of these two peoples has also been the same. As in Greece, so also in India, the rudimentary structure both of the society and the state has always been constitutional and democratic, as distinguished from the military or despotic type of the Semitic races. Their thought-structure, as revealed by the structural peculiarities of their respective languages, is also the same. Language is the expression of thought, and the structure of a language is always determined by the structural peculiarities of the thought of the people among whom that language has been developed. The character of a people's mind is revealed by the position which is assigned in their grammar to the three elements of thought—subject, object and predicate. In the grammatical construction of some languages, the subject dominates the object, in some the object dominates the subject. The absolute domination of the subject over the object in the grammatical structure of any language indicates the essential character of the thought-life of the people by whom, from pre-historic times, that language has been spoken. And this domination means that in the thought of this people the conscionsness of the subject or the self through which the consciousness of the Absolute is evolved and developed among every pepole, has always been very clear and pronounced.

The absolute predominance of the subject over the object is the common character of both Sanskrit and Greek. Nowhere outside the special family of languages, generally called Indo-Aryan, which includes Sanskrit and all the Sanskrit-derived Vernaculars of India on the one hand, and Greek, Latin and the modern languages of Europe on the other,—nowhere outside this group, do we find any thing similar to the significant construction "I am," Sanskrit "Ahamasmi,"—indicating mere existence, simple being, without any reference to doing. And it shows that the sense of being as being, of the subject independent of the object, of the noumenon or the Absolute,—self-existent, self-conditioned, self-determined,—has been an original sense with these peoples. This is the peculiarity of the Aryan thought-sructure. It is a most prominent feature of the Aryan Race-Consciousness. It is the true spiritual sense. It is common to both the Hindu and the Greek; common, therefore, to both Indian and European culture. This strange and rudimentary mental and spiritual affinity between the Greek and the Hindu is proved not merely by the structural similarity of Greek and Sanskrit, but equally also by the general character of all the later and more developed philosophies and arts of these two ancient peoples. Yet there was, inside this wide and fundamental unity, an equally fundamental difference also between their respective mental temperament and spiritual character.

THE PURSUIT OF THE UNIVERSAL.

Both the Greek and the Hindu, you will thus see, have had the same innate sense of the spiritual and the universal as an original endowment of their race-consciousness. This sense of the spiritual and the universal is everywhere expressed through man's perception of the whole. And the whole may be viewed in two ways; we may view it as a concrete Reality, or as an abstract Idea or Principle. In other words, we may view the whole *through* its parts, approach it through the mutual relations of parts to parts, and of the parts, both severally or collectively, to the whole of which they are parts. This is predominantly the way of science. Following this way, we ultimately arrive at what is called the Concrete Universal or the Apara or Saguna Brahman of the Hindus. We may also view the whole *in* the parts. In the true organic conception of the whole, while *actually* it is *revealed through* its parts *logically*, it is equally *implied*, not partially but fully, *in* each one of these parts. The complete thought, though organised in a long and complete sentence, is, however, implicit in each of the words of it. It is the regulative idea that has determined the position of each of these words in the whole sentence. This is the universal character of all organic wholes. We may, therefore, equally seize the whole *in* its parts also. This is predominantly the way of metaphysics. Following this way, we ultimately arrive at what is called the Abstract Universal,—the Para or the Nirguna Brahman of our philosophy. And the pursuit of the Whole or the Absolute through these two different methods, develops two different types of mind.

THE PECULIARITY OF THE GREEK MIND.

In seeking to realise the whole *through* the parts, we have, necessarily to develop and define the relations both severally and collectively, of the parts to the whole of which they are parts. Those who have, from prehistoric times, been used to the pursuit of the whole *through* the parts, have necessarily developed a particular mental temperament. In constantly seeking to seize and define the mutual relations of objects, their mind, as a matter of course, becomes pre-eminently definitive and analytic, objective and realistic. The Greeks followed this way, and these are the distinctive characterstics of the Greek mind. Not that it had no subjectivity or idealism. Every analysis works towards a synthesis every definition suggests a necessary integretion, and no apprehension of the real is really possible except upon a more or less conscious back-ground of the ideal. Greek thought was not therefore, absolutely analytic or definitive or objective or realistic. Both realism and idealism were fully developed in the Greek consciousness. It harmonised the Concrete with the Abstract Universal, even as the Hindus did. But still the dominant emphasis was on the former, and not on the latter. *The* word of Greek culture is, therefore, FORM or DEFINITION.

THE EUROPEAN TEMPEREMENT

Modern Europe is the child of ancient Greece. The characteristic European temperament is fundamentally the same as the Greek temperament. The European mind, even in our own day, is, thus, more prone to define and differentiate than to combine and integrate, more able to analyse than to synthetize; it is more formal than transcendental, more scientific, than metaphysical, more objective than subjective, more positive than imaginative, more realistic than idealistic.

THE PECULIARITY OF THE HINDU MIND.

The Hindu, on the other hand, has, from prehistoric times, followed the opposite way. He has pursued the whole not *through* but *in* the parts. And when we seek the whole *in* the parts, instead of developing we have to deny, instead of positing we have to negate, instead of recognising we have to ignore, the particularities of experience and train the mind to constantly transcend every form of definition and relativity, with a view to reach and realise the Undefinable and the Absolute. It is the way of metaphysics. The Hindu has always followed this way. Not that he never developed any science or philosophy, or that his intellect has been totally devoid of that definitiveness, characterstic of the Greeks. Like the definitive Greek intellect, the Hindu intellect also developed most wonderful systems of grammar and rehtoric, logic and jurispurdence, and even a body of positive science, at a time when it was scarcely known in Europe. His conception of the Concrete Universal or Saguna Brahman, is no less clear, though, perhaps, more full and philosophical, than that of the Greeks. But still, the predominant emphasis cf his thought has been more on the idealistic and the abstract than on the realistic and the concrete.

THE INDIAN TEMPERAMENT.

The resulting mental temperament of the Hindu is, therefore, necessarily more transcendental than formal, more metaphysical than scientific, more imaginative than positive, more idealistic than realistic. And these two fundamentally different types of mental temperaments have created two quite different standards of intellectual and moral values among these two groups of mankind.

TWO DIFFERENT STANDARDS OF VALUES.

With the European, the standard of intellectual, moral and spiritual values is thus, more physical than mental, more external than internal, more sensuous than spiritual. If a European walks from one place to another, he will measure the distance in the terms of miles and furlongs. If he stands before a mountain he will scan its altitude by the theodolite, and express it in relation to the sea-level. If he sees a human being he will psychometrate him, with a view to know his exact proportions. The European can scarcely study even supersensuous facts and experiences except through some sensuous and external help, He seeks to study man's intelligence by measuring his cranium and weighing his brains ; and deduces all his highest generalisations regarding the intellectual or moral advancement of nations and communities from outer statistics and averages. His intellect cannot be satisfied unless all the details, which means the particularities of an object, [are clearly seized and sized and put in their proper place and pose, Even when he rises to the perception of the general he does so by laboriously climbing through the particulars. In the examination or presentation of a thing or theme, neglect of these particularities is to the European an unpardonable intellectual fault.

The Hindu, however, has quite a different standard of intellectual, moral and spiritual values. If he walks from one-place to another, he would oftentimes measure the distance not by chain and compass, but by his own muscles and nerves, and will report it in the terms of his own sensation and emotion. Sometimes, therefore, walking ten miles to meet his friend or lover, he will say that he had only walked a few steps ; on another occasion, when dragged by unpleasant duty or external necessity out of his home to his next-door neighbour, he would, perhaps, say that he had walked five miles. His standard of value is internal not external, intellectual not physical, emotional and not rational in the usual narrow sense of the term. By temperament he has an instinctive and intense distaste of details. By heredity and training he knows only how to seize the universal, to the apparent neglect of isolated particulars. What the European, judging by his own objective and particularistic standard of intellectual or moral or spiritual values, condemns as exaggerations of the Oriental mind are, therefore, really, no exaggerations at all, but are simply the results of a different standard of values. Occasionally even the positive and practical European also adopts this Hindu standard. When a friend meeting a friend after a few weeks says—"I have not seen you for ages,"—he, really, neither exaggerates nor lies, but simply applies his own inner emotional standard to the measurement of outer time. Ordinarily, in regard to events which have little or no reference to his deeper emotions, the European measures time by the swing of the pendulum in his hall-clock. But when his soul is stirred by some deep emotion, whether of love or hatred, then even he ignores, perforce, his habitual standards of outer and objective values, and seizes his own inner self as the only true measure of time, space, and all things besides. And what is, thus, as yet, merely occasional and momentary in the European, is a habitual and permanent characteristic of the Hindu mind : this is, really, all the difference between them.

THE SPOILT CHILD OF MODERN HUMANITY.

I am trying to point out these fundamental psychological differences in the very constitution of the European and the Indian, to explain to you the reason why, in spite of their high education and superior intelligence, even the very best of the European residents or students of India have, almost invariably, failed to truly understand or interpret us. Added to these intellectual difficulties, there are equally serious moral disabilities under which the

European student of Indian character and culture labours. The European is the spoilt child of modern humanity. Every body is humouring him. All the world is praising his wonderful intelligence and acquisitions. Even those who try to verbally deny his superiority, really admit it, by seeking, with all their might, to imitate his ways. He criticises every other culture and civilisation, few have had the temerity to criticise his. He lays down the law of modern life and progress for others but no one has as yet been able to gather up sufficient courage or conceit to lay it down for him. He has sent out his missionaries for the conversion of the world, no one has similarly tried to proseletyze him. All these things have created a strong sense of his own superiority in the European. And this conceit of unquestioned superiority absolutely incapacitates the European from getting a correct understanding of world-cultures different from his own. He recognises these differences. He admits that—

> The East is East and the West is
> West
> And the twain ne'er shall meet.

But all the same, he persistently prefers his own standards of values, as universal standards, by which all the world must be judged. And his claim to interpret us, inspite of this acknowledged difference, means only the claim of the higher, in organic evolution, to explain and interpret the meaning and purpose of the lower!

But if the East be not in reality, only a less developed West, and if there be any truth in the statement that—

> The East is East and the West is
> West
> And the twain ne'er shall meet,

—in other words, if the difference between the very constitutions and structures of these two sections of mankind be so fundamental, as to seem almost as a difference in kind, then, the only possibility of the one section truly understanding the other, must lie in its ability to mentally detach itself from itself, and through the exercise of a highly-developed representative imagination, to spiritually identify itself with the subject of its study and interpretation. But few Europeans have as yet been able to do so.

SISTER NEVEDITA (MISS MARGARET NOBLE.)

The only exception that I know of, was the late Miss Margaret Noble, known and loved all over India, in her adopted name of Sister Nivedita, of the Order of Ramkrishna and Vivekananda. Nivedita's self-effacement was almost complete. Even few Indians, especially of the modern-educated classes, have as yet been inspired by so all-consuming a passion for India, as transfigured this British woman. Nivedita came to us, as no European had as yet come, not as an adept, but as a novice; not as a teacher but as a learner. She did not pose before us as a prophetess but always stood, in sincere love and reverence, as a worshipper. She had no ambition to play the *role* of the high-priestess of any new or old cult. She never claimed any sanctified privilege nor any position of special honour; nor traced any pre-natal connections with our ancient hierarchy, nor ever dabbled in our ancient wisdom, whether open or occult. But in the exuberance of her virgin love for the soul of India, a glimpse of which had been revealed to her by her Guru or Master, she came simply to lose herself in us, and by so losing herself, to find herself back, per chance, as a true seer of our spirit and culture. And her uniqe devotion to our land and people had its reward in the almost complete understanding of some aspects at least of our life and institutions that was vouchsafed unto her. She had, my child, if I am not mistaken, a touch of your own blood in her, and the quick intellectual perceptions and broad spiritual sympathies of her Irish heritage enabled her to see the true Soul of India, where the unimaginative and unsympathetic Englishman or American could rarely peer beyond the outermost covering of her divine body. In her "Web of Indian Life" Sister Nivedita has presented a more correct interpretation of some aspects of our present-day life and thought, than is found in any other English book on India, that I know of.

AN OLD HINDU CANON OF ART.

The fact of the matter is that no one can correctly interpret anything without himself becoming that thing. It is true not only of the interpretation of men, but even of animals and vegetables. This truth had been seized ages ago by us, and it is an old canon of Hindu Art that to correctly draw or paint an object, the artist must first himself become that object; for, the true function of the painter's or the sculptor's art is not merely to reproduce with absolute fidelity the *forms* of things, which may very well be done by any trained photographer, but to reveal their inner soul or being. And the complete mental and spiritual identification of the artist with his subject, is the only way to reach this ideal. To correctly present India, one must, therefore, first be himself an Indian, not merely by birth, but in heart and in spirit. But such self-effacement is almost impossible of attainment by the ordinary European; for the European, my child, can never cease to be an European, nay not even in imagination.

TRUE NIRVANA: WHAT IT MEANS.

It has, however, been always very different with the Hindu. A most powerful and uniqe representative imagination has been the special heritage of our race. It is the fruit of our age-long social and spiritual disciplines. To kill the conceit of self, as a thing apart and thus to seize the universal everywhere,—this has been the one eternal objective of all our evolution and culture. Our rituals and sacraments, our fasts and feasts, our social regulations and religious liturgies, all have had, from time immemorial, this one end in view, namely, to help the realisation of the Absolute through the conscious spiritual identification of the individual self with the Universal. Our highest conception of salvation is, therefore, called, *Brahma Nirvana*, which means, not the annihilation of self-consciousness, but only the conscious and spiritual identification of the individual with the Universal, through transcending all the carnal limitations of the human personality. The true Yogi, says Sree Krishna in the Bhagabad-Geeta, "sees the self (his own self) in all things, and sees all things in the self"; and thus losing the conceit of independent and isolated personality, he attains the vision of the Universal.

He who sees Me everywhere, and sees everything in Me,
I never pass out of his sight, nor does he ever pass out of Mine.

This is the true and positive conception of nirvana. It is a universal Hindu ideal. Realising the identity of his own self with the Universal, the sage Bamadeva, we are told in the Vedas, declared—"I am the Sun, I was Manu." Every true Hindu devotee pursues this self-same ideal even to-day, and some at least, actually attain it.

BABA ARJOONDAS.

Such a holy man was present, some years ago, at the great Kumbha-Fair at Allahabad. These fairs that are held every twelve years, at such centres of Hinduism as Hardwar near the source of the Ganges, or Allahabad at the junction of the Jumna and the Ganges or Nasik on the Godaveri, are like great religious congresses, where the holy mendicants and devotees of India periodically assemble, and spend a few weeks in cultivating mutual acquaintance and exchaging spiritual offices with one another. Baba Arjoondas, one of the most-renowned of the Hindu saints of our day, was present at the Kumbha of 1894-95. Those who have seen him know how he lives in a perpetual consciousness of the Universal. He is a devotee of Rama, one of the incarnations of Vishnu or the Supreme Lord according to the sacred traditions of the Hindus;—and he sees his Rama in every human being. He once came to Calcutta. It was during the hot summer days. A friend of mine went to see him. The day was very sultry and my friend was literally bathed in perspiration as he walked up the stairs of the house where Arjoondas was living. Immediately he saw my friend, Baba Arjoondas came up to him, and commenced actually to adore him, after the manner of the Hindus, by devoutly moving the right palm before his face and all the time repeating to himself his favourite formula—"O! my darling Rama! O! my darling Rama!" This devout greeting over, the Baba took up a fan and for full one hour and a quarter fanned my friend, with the loving tenderness with which the mother fans the tired and perspiring limbs of her dearly beloved son. And all this time he was explaining the methods and disciplines of the Bhakti-Yoga, or union with God through love and faith, citing copious texts not only from ancient Sanskrit scriptures but also from the vernacular literature of Upper India. To the spiritual vision of this devout Hindu, there is really no such thing as mere man. In every human he realises his Rama, the Incarnation of Vishnu or the Supreme Lord, according to the Hindu Vaishnavas. Indeed, Baba Arjoondas seeks to reach out to the loftiest conception of Humanity through his beloved Rama, even as the truly illumined Christian tries to reach through his beloved Christ; though, perhaps the emotional and spiritual moods of the Hindu are deeper and more varied than those of the Christian. Baba Arjoondas never can see any evil in any man, not even in those who are diametrically opposed, in their life and habits, to himself. Another friend of mine was once walking along the street with Arjoondas, and seeing a European, on the way, the Baba wanted to know who he was. My friend, to test the universality of the Baba's love and humanity, spoke very deprecatingly of the European, saying that he was a Mleccha, an unclean person, who had no holiness in him and who ate and drank everything with everybody. At this Baba Arjoondass enthusiastically exclaimed, his face beaming with loving admiration:—"What great love have they, what great love! They eat and drink with everybody, Oh my darling Ram,—what great love is here!". Yet Baba Arjoondass, and the type he represents, would be described as a heathen, and an idolator by many a European observer, both lay and missionary, though those who have come in contact with the Baba declare that there is greater spirituality and a deeper and more living God-consciousness in the so-called idolatry of this Vaishnava devotee, than is found in all the aggressive and dogmatic missionary religions of the world, which claim the exclusive privilege of worshipping the One True God, in spirit and in truth !

"NOT THIS ME: BUT ANOTHER ME."

Baba Arjoondas was present at the Kumbha-Fair at Allahabad in 1894-95. One day a friend of mine saw him crying on the road-side, saying that he had been thrashed by a policeman. This very much upset my friend. Such an outrage was unthinkable even in India, and he begged Baba Arjoondas to point out to him the man who had committed this cowardly sacrilege. They both walked along the road for some time, the Baba crying all the while, until a policeman was found. My friend now asked Baba Arjoondas, if this was the offending officer. At this the Baba seemed to come back to himself, and said—"The policeman beat, "not this me" but "another me."

ANOTHER HOLY MAN.

Hindu saints and devotees cultivate their sympathetic imagination not only in regard to men, but equally also in regard to the lower animals and even in regard to vegetables. All that have sentiency are included in the term *jeeba*. Man and animals and vegetables are all *jeebas*, in Sanskrit. And love of the *jeeba* is a universal Hindu ideal. In seeking to realise it, our saints and devotees always cultivate what may be called a kind of vicarious identity with all these. Their love of men is, thus, of the same class as their love of self. Their love of animals and vegetables is again, of the same class as their love of men. There is, thus, almost an element of personal romance in their love of nature, as well as in their love of men. Their enjoyment of the beauties of birds and beasts and of flowers and plants has, therefore, more than a mere æsthetic reference, it is supremely spiritual. They not only love, but actually lose themselves sometimes in both animals and vegetables as much as they do in other humans like themselves. Such a holy man was living, many years ago, at Kalighat, in the outskirts of Calcutta. The capacity for vicarous sufferings and enjoyments had been very exceptionally developed, even for a Hindu devotee, in this saintly man. Many a time, while walking along the streets of this modern suburb, if he happened to see any poor woman, sitting by the road side or in her hut or shop nursing her baby, this holy man would lose all consciousness of his individuality in the suckling baby, and going to its mother would gently push it aside, and placing his hoary head on her lap, would commence to behave with her as if she was his own mother, and he her baby boy. The same transfiguration happened also, occasionally, in regard to the other sacred emotions. But the peculiarity of his type of spirituality was his almost complete identification even with the animal and the vegetable kingdoms. One day a stray bull entered his garden and commenced to eat up his flowers and plants. Moved by love for the vegetables he rushed out, stick in hand, to drive the intruder away. But when he went near it, and saw how the bull was enjoying its excellent feast, he stood dumb and motionless, tears flowing from his eyes. On the one hand he felt in his own self the intense pain of the vegetables at the loss of their tender leaves and shoots, on the other hand he simultaneously felt also the deep satisfaction of the bull equally in his own soul. And torn between these two conflicting emotions, he did not know what to do. The conflict became almost unbearable to him, and, as he expained to a devoted visitor,—torn by it, his heart cried out—"Oh God, why should there be this cruel antagonism in thy creation so that the happiness and enjoyment of one class or individual can only be secured through the misery and deprivation of another!"

AN ACTUAL "SUPER-MAN."

They talk and write, as you know, a lot of fanciful nonsense in Europe of the coming super-man. Judging from the picture drawn of him by some at least of your writers, this super-man seems to me to mean only a superior animal. When you come however to India, my child, you will see what this super-man truly is. He belongs to the class of which I have been speaking here. We do not call them super-men. In our language and literature they are called—*Jeebanmooktas*, which literally means, emancipated-in-life. They are freed from all bondage, physical, intellectual and moral, even in this life. Not that the body absolutely ceases to be subject to physical laws and conditions, or that the intellect or the conscience ceases to work naturally; but only this that the *Jeebanmooktas* are able to transcend, at their will, the mental and spiritual limitations, which our senses and our intellect impose upon us. They are able, it is said, to transcend outer physical limitations as well.

PANDIT BIJOY KRISHNA GOSWAMI.

I have myself had the supreme good fortune of sitting at the feet of a holy man, Pandit Bijoy Krishna Goswami, who had actually attained this supreme spiritual ideal. He was a Bengalee. In early youth he had fallen in with the movement of social and religious reform and freedom in India, known as the Brahma Samaj. Along with Maharshi Debendra Nath Tagore and Babu Keshub Chunder Sen, Bijoy Krishna Goswami also held the highest position

৺শ্রীশ্রীরামকৃষ্ণ পরম হংস দেব

Mohila Press Calcutta

among the pioneers of this great movement. In later life he fully attained the high spiritual state described as Brahma-Nirvana in our books. He was a living super-man, a true example of the Jeebanmookta. We read in the Upanishads that the devotee who has seen the Supreme, has had "all the knots of his heart cut through (*i.e*, all his self-regarding desires absolutely killed), all his spiritual doubts completely dispelled, and all his karma (*i.e*, the seeds of all possible self-regarding activities in the future, whether here or here-after) absolutely worn out." This is our ideal of the superman. This is the real thing, which the modern fancy has commenced to speak of as "Beyond Good and Evil". Pandit Bijoy Krishna Goswami, like his saintly contemporary, Paramhansa Ramkrishna,—a very meagre and imperfect sketch of whom was given out to the English-speaking world some years ago by Professor Max Muller,—had attained this state. He had killed all conceit of self in him. His spiritual detatchment from his body and his senses was complete. In moments of illness he used always to say that it was the body only which suffered for its own karma—the conscious or unconscious violation of the laws of health,—but these sufferings did not, in the least, affect his mind and soul. Upon the death of his saintly wife, he wrote to his daughter—"Your mother has gone to the other world. It is not proper to grieve for her, but rather rejoice." The thin partition that divides the here from the hereafter had no existence in his spiritual vision. When his younger daughter died, though he had been exceedingly fond of her, instead of any depression, those who were about him saw a strange transfiguration in him. It was like Christ's vision of Eliza. Every death in his family seemed, indeed, to open afresh the portals of the holy spirit-world to his vision. Nor death nor life made any real difference to him. His disciplined and illumined spirit had actually learnt to transcend both time and space. Near or far, presence or absence, were the same to him. Neither health nor disease, nor wealth nor proverty, nor adulation nor abuse, nor fame nor shame, made the least little difference to this saintly Bengalee. All religions were the same to him,—the revelations of his God. All sects were the same to him, who claimed no special relations with any. All men were the same to him,—the image of God, the Temple of the Deity. In his life and conversation one could see the loftiest and the most transcendental teachings of our ancient scriptures visibly verified. Yet, there was little or nothing of so-called supernaturalism in him. Not that he absolutely disbelieved the supernatural, but only this, that in the spirit of ancient Hindu seers and sages, he always condemned all "signs and wonders," as a hindrance to the attainment of the highest love and faith. Many an English-educated Indian, who, in the name of science and reason, had at one time dismissed his national scriptures as fanciful and false, got back the lost faith, by coming in contact with this holy man, and by thus seeing these old records verified in his life and character.

Like Baba Arjoondas, Pandit Bijoy Krishna Goswami also, inspite of his early modernism and rationalism, had developed a most wonderful sympathetic imagination. To see any keen human suffering was, for him, to have it directly transferred to his own sensations. One wintry morning he was sitting in his usual place, in the Brahma Samaj Mission House, at Dacca, facing the garden, beyond which was the public road. All of a sudden he seemed to take ill with a severe fit of shivering. His people did not know what it meant, or what to do. A disciple, however, noticed that his eyes were fixed on a decrepit old beggar seated on the footpath on the other side of the public road, who was shivering in all his bare limbs at the touch of the sharp and frosty morning breeze. He at once took the heavy blankets that covered the Master's body, and running out to the street, put it round the old beggar. As soon as this was done, the Master came back to himself, and all his shivering ceased.

It was not the only incident of its kind in the life of this saintly Hindu. The experience was repeated, so far as there is any record, once at Durbhanga in Behar, and again at Allahabad in the winter of 1894-95 where Bijoy Krishna Goswami had gone to attend the Kumbha-Fair.

THE TRUE INDIAN PROTO-TYPE.

It is these holy men of India, my child, both Hindu and Mahomedan, who furnish us with the right key to the interpretation of Indian life and institutions. They are the genuine products of the soil. They are the finest fruits of our social and religious institutions. In them the highest possibilities of the special thought and culture of our land have been fully brought out. It is these holy men who have, from generation to generation, maintained the essential continuity of our culture, while progressively adjusting our socio-religious life and institutions to the changing conditions, both physical and social, of their people. There is no life-less formalism or hide-bound conservatism in these men. Their illumined intellect and absolutely self-less lives enabled them from age to age to initiate social and religious progress without the violent revolts through which the social and religious evolution of Europe has uniformly sought to work itself out. Rising above all personal passions and prejudices and all carnal conflicts between the individualities and particularities of social life and religious opinions, and in every way thus identifying themselves with the universal, they have been able to harmonise order with progress and prevent the growth of the spirit of revolution and anarchy in their community. It is to these men that we owe all the peculiar developments of our social, our moral, and our religious life. In Europe the history of socio-ethical evolution has been different from that in India. From Status, through the revolt of Right, to the highest ideal of Duty, in the modern sense of complete and perfect self-realisation through the faithful discharge of the obligations imposed upon the individual by his station in life,—this has been the scheme of socio-ethical evolution in Christendom. In India, owing to the peculiar synthetic genius of the race and the control of the course of social evolution, not by rebels and reformers but by its spirit-illumined saints and sages, the scheme of socio-ethical evolution has been directly *from* Status *to* Duty for its own sake. Similarly, the evolution of religion in India has also been fundamentally different from that of Europe. In the earliest stage religion is ethnic, miscalled national by some European students of religious history. Judaism, the tribal religions of Arabia before the birth of Islam, as well as the earliest forms of our own Vedic religion, all belong to this ethnic type. From the ethnic stage, religious evolution, both in Christendom and in Islam, passed through a credal stage to true universalism. The evolution of religion in India somehow skipped over the intermediate stage of credalism. Hinduism has never been a credal religion. The Budhistic protest did develop a creed, and, as it seems to me, on account of this very credal character, the spirit of Hinduism threw out Buddhism, as every strong and healthy organism throws out a foreign body that accidentally enters into it.

And these peculiarities in our history and evolution are, as it seems to me, entirely due to the controlling influence exercised over the course of our socio-religious evolution, by successive generations of our holy men. They are the true proto-types of Indian humanity. A tree must not only be judged by its fruit but should also be interpreted by it. The child should be interpreted by the man, and not the man by the child. The meaning of the individuals belonging to a type, must be sought for and found in its proto-type. It is, therefore, that if you really desire to correctly understand and truly appreciate our life and culture, you must seek, my child, first and foremost of all to study, to love, and thus to understand the holy men of India.

CHARACTERISTICS OF THE INDIAN IDEAL.

Absolute self-detachment and a most unique and lofty idealism are the main characteristics of these holy men.

These are the essential elements of the true spiritual life, as we in India have always understood it. And it is here, in this detachment and idealism, that you must seek for the right key to the correct interpretation of all the apparent perplexities of our social institutions and religious life. It is on account of this detachment and this idealism that a community controlled by a most rigid system of castes rarely suffered from class-war or developed any violent spirit of mutual jealousy or recrimination in its members, until we commenced, very recently, to improve and reform it by the individualistic and capitalistic competitive class-distinctions of the imported socio-political ideals of modern European civilisation. In our old caste-life, there was no conscious conceit of superiority in the so-called higher and, therefore, no rankling sense of inferiority in the so-called lower castes, and this was due to the spirit of detachment that has stood at the back, not always of our conscious, but certainly, of our sub-conscious life. And we should always remember that the elements of our sub-conscious life furnish far stronger proofs of our real character than the conventionalities and artificialities that constitute so large a portion of what we call our conscious life.

And if our spirit of detatchment saved our society from the ugly rivalries of the competitive class-distinctions of Europe, our idealism always helped us to transcend all forms of social irregularities, due to convention or culture, and realise the Divine as much in the holy Brahmin as in the untouchable Pariah.

DHARMA—THE BASIS OF OUR CIVILISATION.

These two fundamental characteristics of our culture, detachment and idealism, have been combined into an organic whole, in our conception of Dharma, loosely rendered by the

English word religion. Strictly speaking, the concept is untranslatable. There is, no doubt, some slight affinity between the radical meaning of the two words :—Dharma, being derived from Sanskrit *dhri* to hold and Religion from Latin *ligare* to bind. Dharma is that which holds together the different elements of a thing and thus combines them into one organic whole. Religion is that which binds men together. The conception of religion is, thus, exclusively human and social ; that of dharma is cosmic and universal. The elementals have no religion. We can never speak of the religion of fire, or water, or ether or air. But we always speak in Sanskrit, and all the Sanskrit-derived vernaculars of India, of the dharma of these elementals. Heat is, thus, the dharma of fire, coolness of water, sound of ether, motion of air. Everything in creation has its dharma. The most correct rendering of our dharma is to be found in your word Law—with a capital "L". It is Law in the specific Emersonian sense,—the Law of Being. And as every object, whether animate or inanimate,—whether vegetable or animal or human—has its own law of being, so we can reasonably use the word dharma in regard to them all.

This Law or Law of Being is not, however, imposed upon objects from without, but grows from within, through the general course of their history and evolution. It is what, in the philosophy of evolution, they call a Regulative Idea. It is something constitutional. And as the constitutions of different things differ, so this dharma also organises and expresses itself differently in different objects. As there are constitutional differences between one individual human and another, so the dharma of one man cannot truly be the dharma of another. It is something essentially specific and personal. The law and course of ethical and spiritual evolution in one person, cannot, therefore, be necessarily the same as that of another. What is good for one, may not, therefore, be good for another. There must consequently be great diversities of both faiths and cultures in the community, owing to fundamental constitutional differences between the individuals composing it. Hinduism has always recognised this fact. It is, therefore, not one religion, like Christianity or Islam, but a federation of many cults and cultures. The Hindu society is also, for the same reason, not a homogeneous unit but rather a highly developed organic whole which seeks to realise its essential unity not by denying but openly accepting and harmonising in the totality of its life, the endless diversities of its component organisms. Like the Hindu religion Hindu society is also not a unit but a federation of many units. The freedom and integrity of the parts inside the unity of the whole, is the very soul and essence of the federal idea. And in no religion or society that I know of, has this organic federal ideal being sought to be so fully realised as in the Hindu religion and the Hindu society.

And because of this wonderful combination of isolation and association, of freedom and federation, in the very constitution of our society and religion, you find that in a country inhabited by so many different races, racial antagonism has scarcely been known; and among a people divided into so many sects and cults never had the stake or the rack been set up for the spiritual benefit of the heretic.

The word of Indian Evolution is Dharma; the word of European Evolution is Right. And these two words seem, to my mind, to completely sum up the fundamental difference between India and Europe. Dharma is the law of renunciation, Right is the law of resistance. Dharma demands self-abnegation, Right self-assertion. Dharma developes collectivism: Right individualism. Dharma works for synthesis: Right lives and grows in antethesis. Dharma is the soul of order: Right the parent of revolution. To understand India we must seize the conception of Dharma. To understand Europe we must seize the principle of Right. How then, can the generalisations of European experience, gathered under the Law of Right, help one to interpret the character and culture of India trained in the Ideal of Dharma?

India, my child, must therefore, interpret herself.

LETTER II.

THE NAME AND THE THING.

PERSONAL AND PREFATORY.

I am very glad, indeed, that you liked my last letter. I was rather afraid that you would find it tediously long, and, in places, rather dry and abstruse. Of course I could not help it. I have had to clear the ground, and state the reasons why India has not yet been understood by Europe. The fact that, inspite of its length and abstruseness, you found it, as you say, so "entrancingly" interesting, proves, however, not the quality of my exposition, but only the strength of your love of India. I am exceedingly gratified to find this fresh proof of your romantic admiration for our country and culture. It is the surest of all assurances that sooner or later you will be able to understand us such as but few foreigners have as yet been able to do.

THE TRUE INTERPRETER.

You want me to undertake the work of interpreting India to the modern world. You know not, my child, what you are asking for. I do not possess, as my friends know, any excess of humility in my composition. But with all my conceit, I dare not claim the intellectual and spiritual qualifications necessary in a true interpreter of India. My vision of India is yet rather dim and hazy. It specially lacks that definiteness of details so essential to every faithful and illuminating picture. I am only feeling after her. Not to speak of myself, I know only two or three persons, among all our most intelligent and highly educated classes, who have had the fullest equipment for this work. Some may claim wide scholarship, the fruit of laborious study and research, but lack that consuming passion for their country and culture, without which the soul of things can never be seized. Others may have a kind of native love for their own land and people, but lack large scholarship and deep insight. The interpreter must be absolutely possessed by the spirit of the thing he seeks to interpret. But can we, of the present generation in India, claim this possession? We are much too completely possessed by the spirit of modern Europe, to be effectually seized by the real spirit of India. We are the fruits of a hybrid education that has produced a kind of intellectual and spiritual atavism in us. This education has, on the one hand, divorced our mind and spirit from the deeper realities of the life and thought of our own country, without, on the other hand, placing us in any living and real relations even with the life and thought of Europe. We scarcely understand Europe, however, much we may ape her ways. We cannot understand India, however much we may swear aloud by her name. How then shall we be able to interpret her?

THE "REFORMER" AND THE "REACTIONARY."

Broadly speaking, we, the so-called modern-educated classes of India, stand divided into two opposite camps. Some are "reformers," some are "reactionaries." But neither of these have, to my mind, any real and correct appreciation of their own country and culture. The "reformer" applying the untested canons of imported European enlightenment, to the examination of the surface values of Indian life and institutions, sees signs of almost universal degradation and decadence about him. India may have been great and noble, wise and strong, pious and pure, at one time. But now she is mean and ignoble, ignorant and weak, godless and vicious. This is the ordinary reformer's estimate of his own country and culture. You might as legitimately go to him for a correct understanding of Indian life and institutions as you might seek the Mahomedan Moulavi for a faithful and illuminating interpretation of Hindu ritualism or the Christian Trinity. The standard of judgment which the reformer applies to the examination of his own country and culture, in passing his cruel verdict on them, is derived neither from the rational generalisations of the course of history and evolution in India itself, nor even from those of universal history and culture, but from the crude conclusions of European empiricism. European society is democratic, the Indian patriarchal. The latter is, therefore, necessarily lower than the former. There is considerable latitude of social intercourse in Europe, in India it is hedged in by multitudinous restrictions of sex and caste. India is, therefore, fundamentally inferior to Europe in the matter of social progress. In Europe the masses are, to a large extent, literate, and therefore, educated. In India they are illiterate and necessarily uneducated and unintelligent. This is the general way in which the reformer examines and judges India. Judging them in the light of the history and acheivements of Europe, he constantly condemns his own country and culture, and with the relentless pity of the missionary propagandist seeks to ruthlessly improve them more or less after these alien ideals.

The "reactionary" from a different motive, and pursuing quite an opposite method, also applies unconsciously the standards of Europe, not to abolish but rather to revive and re-establish the social and religious institutions of his country. In religion, the reactionary is setting up for the Indian scriptures the same claims to infallibility and absolutism, that credal systems like Christianity or Islam popularly claim for the Bible or the Koran. He forgets that neither verbal infallibility nor any exclusive and absolute authority had ever been vested in the religious scriptures of Hinduism. In sociology, the reactionary tries to revive the relaxing rigidities of the Indian caste-system in the spirit of the class domination of Europe; and, thereby, he ignores the patent fact that the genius of the Indian caste-system never tolerated this spirit of domination in the so-called higher, and consequently, rarely evoked any spirit of envious revolt in the so-called lower castes. Conceit of superiority has been uniformly condemned in the higher castes ; while, the almost absolute autonomy enjoyed by the different castes in regard to all matters concerning their caste-life, and the sense of mutual interdependence cultivated in all the castes, both higher and lower, as limbs and organs of a great organic whole,—left, indeed, but little room for the growth of such conceits. The reactionary is, thus, as much under the spell of European ideas and ideals as the reformer. The only difference between them is that while the reformer is trying to consciously control and regulate his social evolution after the manner of Europe, the reactionary is unconscious of the domination of these alien ideas. The strange psychological affinity between these two rival camps will be clearly realised when we remember that there are only two ways of intellectual and spiritual appropriation. One is the way of love, the other of hatred; for love and hatred both—and hatred, perhaps, even more than love,—help us to be possessed by the thing we love or hate. In love as well as in hatred there is deep concentration of the mind on the object of our emotion. And we always unconsciously become that which we constantly think of. The reformer becomes Europeanised by his love, the reactionary by his hatred, of European ideals and institutions.

Both the reformer and the reactionary are, thus, found at the final analysis, to be equally inspired, the one consciously, and the other unconsciously, by the spirit of Europe. Both have, more or less, imbibed the European temperament. Both are, though in different ways, emphatically objective and materialistic. The one is dominated by individualistic ethicism, the other by effete formalism; and both these equally lack that true inwardness which is characteristic of the thought and culture of India. The one revels in the unrealities of subjective abstractions; the other in the unrealities of effete and ununderstood rituals. The reformer by his unillumined and empirical criticism of our life and institutions strengthens the forces of reaction in the country; while the reactionary by the infidel tenacity with which he is seeking to hold on to the lifeless and decadent forms of our social and religious life, lends strength and vitality to the reformer's revolt. And in their mutual wranglings and recriminations, the perception of the true Soul of India is lost. You will find the real truth about India in the presentation of neither of these two classes. It lies really in the traditional "Middle-Path" of the sage and the philosopher. I am only a humble enquirer, my child, seeking light and guidance into that Holy Path. How can I dare to pose as a guide to others?

But though I dare not accept the holy office of the interpreter of India, I may well, and quite legitimately, undertake to study and understand her. It is, indeed, not only the high privilege, but a distinct duty, of even the least of her children, to try to understand her through reverent and diligent study and investigation. This much, my child, I can, and will do for you: and if it should in any way help you to a better and deeper understanding and appreciation of our culture and civilisation than what you have now, I shall thankfully consider all my labours more than amply repaid.

INDIA AS SEEN BY THE STRANGER.

To begin, then, from the very name of India, we have to remember that this name was given her not by her own children, but by the stranger within her gate. We never called her either India or Hindoostan. We knew her of old by quite a different name.

The stranger came to us, in the early days of our history, by our north-western land-route. This is the way that the Babylonians and the Assyrians, the Persians, and, later, the Greeks also, came to us. In seeking to do so they had to cross a great river. Our own native name for that great river was Sindhu. It is still known among us by that ancient name. The sibilant "S" of our Sindhu became, however, the aspirant "H" in the tongue of the Babylonians and Persians. Our Sindhu became their Hindu. You would do well to remember that the original reference of this word Hindu was not to our religion, but simply to one of our great rivers. The Hindu of the Babylonians and Persians became then the Indus of the Greeks and the Romans. The land of the Indus became India.

INDIA A MERE "GEOGRAPHICAL EXPRESSION".

In its origin and history India is, thus, truly and really what the present day European, either from ignorance or pride, is so anxious to prove. It is undoubtedly a mere geographical expression. It indicates simply a distinctive geographical feature of the country. In fact the geographical boundaries of this land are so peculiar and prominent, that we cannot blame the stranger if he be so profoundly impressed by them as to entirely forget or ignore its more fundamental and significant features. The Himalayas on the north, and the sea on the south, as well as practically also towards the east and the west of the Peninsula, demarcate this land from the rest of the Asiatic Continent. Both these are most prominent physical features of the country. Such boundaries are scarcely found anywhere in our known world, except in relation to what we call continents. The physical isolation of India is really continental. So also is the immense extent of her territory. She has the largest surface area of any country in the world, China, Russia, and the United States excepted. The total area of India is nearly one-third of that of the continent of Europe. It is nearly fourteen times as large as Great Britain, and over ten times the size of the entire British Isles. It is a good deal over five times the area of Austria-Hungary, and more than six times that of either France or Germany. So immense a tract of territory, covering so many latitudes and longitudes, must naturally have quite a variety of physical and physiographical features also. It is a land of many altitudes and many climates. In some places you will find the suffocating heat of the tropics, in others the more pleasant and equable temperatures of the true temperate zones: while there are places in India where you may find as much snow and frost in the winter months, as the heart of the most homesick Englishman or Scotchman may be pining for. There are provinces in India where we have the highest records of the world's rainfall, as in the Kasi Hills; while in some other places as Sindh, there is hardly any rainfall from year's end to year's end. With such diversities of physical and physiographical conditions and characters, it is only natural that India should have an equally large variety of both flora and fauna. Both in its physical features, and in the wealth and variety of its vegetable and animal kingdoms, this extensive tract of territory is truly continental. It is equally large and diversified in its human populations also. The total strength of our population counts one-fifth of the whole human race. We have the largest population of any country in the world, with the exception of the Chinese Empire. We are over ten times as many as the English and the Welsh combined, nine times as many as the French, six times as many as the Germans, four times as many as the Americans, and quite three times as many as the Russians. In this huge mass of humanity almost all the great racial varieties of mankind are more or less represented. The main body of the population is of undoubted Aryan origin, though there has been considerable admixture with other races, during the many thousand years that have elapsed since the Aryans first settled in this country. The Dravidians dominate the populations of the southern part of the Peninsula, while there is an unmistakable Mongolian element in the populations of the north-eastern provinces. There is an equally strong Nigriting element among the dark aboriginal races; while the Semitic blood dominates a very large percentage of that higher section of the Moslem community in India, who, like the Normans in England, came over to us with the Mahomedan conquest. This teeming population, composed of different original racialities, speak many languages, profess many faiths, and obey many social and sacerdotal laws and customs. And all these bewildering diversities of racial origin, as well as of languages and literatures, and cults and customs, combine to strengthen the first impression produced by the physical characteristics of the land upon the uninitiated stranger, namely, that it is not a country but a continent.

THE POPULAR ANGLO-INDIAN VIEW.

This is, really, the most popular and prevailing view of India in Europe and America. The European or American visitor to India comes to us with this strong prepossession, and all his outer experience of our country and people, instead of dissipating, helps, on the contrary, to confirm and strengthen this view. He cannot discover any fundamental principle of unity at the back of these bewildering diversities, except perhaps that new administrative, political, social, and economic unity which the establishment of the British Empire has been working in our own time. Every Anglo-Indian publicist assiduously proclaims that India is not a country but a collection of countries, which have as little or as much in common with one another, either in race or history, as the German, the French, the Dutch, the Russian, the Italian, the English and the Spaniard in Europe have between them. It would be as correct, they declare, to view Europe as one country and the different nations of that great Continent as one nation or people as it would be to regard India as one land, and the so-called Indians as one people. In fact there is no such thing as an Indian: there are Bengalees, and Marhattas, and Tamils and Telegus and Shiks and Goorkhas, Mahomedans and Jains, and Buddhists, but really no Indians: in any case, there never was such an animal as Indian, until the British rulers of the country commenced so generously to manufacture him with the help of their schools and their colleges, their courts and their camps, their law and their administration, and their free press and open platform. This is also the orthodox official view of India, that finds repeated utterance and authoritative exposition from responsible Anglo-Indian rulers and prominent British politicians. Nor can it be denied that there is a very large element, not of truth, but surely of very strong plausibility in this popular and orthodox official view. The fact of the matter really is, that as long as you look upon our country as "India, or the Land of the Indus"—you will get no closer and truer view of it than what the foreign officials and students have been able to do.

INDIA AS KNOWN TO HER OWN CHILDREN.

But while the stranger called her India, or the Land of the Indus, thereby emphasising only her strange physical features, her own children, from of old, have known and loved her by another name. We never called her India. Long before the Greek invasion and even before tne Babylonians and Assyrians came in any sort of close contact with us, we had given this name to our country. That name is Bharatavarsha. To clearly understand and grasp the nature and reality of the fundamental unity in which all our divergent and even apparently conflicting characters and customs, cults and cultures, our racialities and provincialities, have almost from the very beginning of our history, been rationally reconciled, you must try to realise the deep significance of this old and native name of the land which the foreigner has so long called and known as India.

MEANING OF GEOGRAPHICAL NAMES.

Geographical names belong to three classes: some have a mere physical origin and reference, some have an ethnic or tribal origin and reference, and some, much fewer in number, have what may be called a personal and historic origin and reference. Names like the Transvaal, derived from the river Vaal, and India, from the river Indus, belong to the first class. Aryavarta, the old name of what is now known as Upper India, derived from the Aryas or Aryans who settled there, and England from the Angles, belong to the second or the ethnic group. Rome from Romulus, and Bharatavarsha from Bharata, these belong to the third and historic group of geographical names. And wherever a country is commenced to be called after some great historic personage, especially some great king or potentate, whether real or legendary, there necessarily lies at the back of it a distinct historic or national consciousness. Rome did not connote any geographical features of the city or principality that received this name, nor any tribality of its people, nor even any religious unity or affinity that might have existed among them, but predominantly, and even exclusively, an individual civic or national entity. It had, of course, like all other places under human habitation, its physicalities and its tribalities, its socialities and its religiosities: but the particular name by which it came to be known among men, referred to none of these, but prominently and almost exclusively, to what may be called its civic unity or national individuality. Her name itself was the most conclusive proof that Rome was not a mere geographical entity, or the habitat of a particular tribe or groups of tribes, but had developed a distinct national consciousness.

THE MEANING OF BHARATAVARSHA.

Those who so persistently deny any fundamental historic unity or any real national individuality to our land and our people, either do not know, or they do not remember the fact that we never called our country by the alien name of India or even by that of Hindoostan. Our own name was, and is still today, among the Aryan populations of the country, Bharatavarsha. And Bharatavarsha is not a physical name like India or the Transvaal, nor even a tribal or ethnic name like England or Aryavarta, but a distinct and unmistakable historic name like Rome. It is derived from Bharata. This Bharata is as much a historic personage as Romulus. Strictly speaking, both Bharata and Romulus are more legendary than, perhaps, historical.

But the profound significance of the name which they gave to these two great countries of the ancient world, is by no means affected by their legendary or even mythical character. India may not be one country but a collection of countries confined within certain prominent physical boundaries. It may be peopled by many races speaking many languages, professing many religions, owning many cultures. But those who gave it one common name must have realised some fundamental unity at the back of all these endless diversities. Men never call any collection of things of divergent character or properties by one single name, unless they are able to seize some prominent and undeniable principle of unity in them. Those who gave the name of Bharatavarsha to India must have done so. And the unity that they seized behind the diversities of the life of their country was not a mere physical or even a mere tribal or ethnic unity, like that which is indicated by such geographical names as India or Aryavarta; but was an essential historic or national unity as is connoted by the name Rome. India was then, as it is now, divided into many provinces, inhabited by many peoples with their peculiar cultures and characteristics, represented many faiths and cults, had many languages and literatures. And yet all these endless diversities notwithstanding, it was called by one common name. And this fact conclusively proves the presence of some undeniable principle of historic or national unity in the consciousness of the people or peoples who lived in this land even in those early days.

THE CHARACTER OF INDIAN UNITY.

What, then, was the real character of this Indian Unity? Bharata was, like Romulus, a king. He is a Vedic personage. Though described as the lord and master of the "world with all the seas," it cannot be held that he was the real ruler of even all the territories that received his name, and came to be called his "varsha." The limit of Bharatavarsha extended in those days even much further than the present limits of India. Balk, called in our ancient books Balhik, and Kandahar, our old Gandhar, were among its north-western provinces. Towards the east, Bharatavarsha extended as far as the very confines of the modern Chinese Empire, and included both the modern Upper and Lower Burma. It is incredible that in those early days, all this extensive tract was subject to one single king or emperor. In fact, such political sovereignty or administrative centralisation as would be implied by any hypothesis of this character, was absolutely foreign to the very genius of the Aryan people of India. Even at the time of the Mahabharata, which was much later than that of this Bharata from whom our land derived its significant name, it was not in any sense a political and administrative unit like the present British Empire in India. The epithets applied to King Bharata are also quite impartially applied to many other great kings who figured at the great Bharata War. Every powerful monarch is described in our old books as lord and master of the whole world. Bharata was, undoubtedly, a great king. He is described as a *raja-ckakravarti*, very loosely rendered into English, sometimes, by the word emperor. But neither Bharata, nor, indeed, any of the great monarchs spoken of in the old books, was an emperor in the modern sense. Modern empires have grown through conquests and appropriations of the lands of other sovereigns. But we scarcely find any evidence of such earth-hunger in our old kings and warriors. Kings no doubt fought with one another: but it was very rarely indeed that the victor appropriated to himself the territories of the vanquished. The usual practice, on the contrary, was to place some son or relation of the defeated monarch upon his throne, even where, for any reason, the vanquished, if still living, could not be placed back into his old position and authority. The Hindu *rajachakravarti* was, therefore, not an emperor, as he is known in Europe, but was simply the nominal head of a friendly federation of kingdoms and principalities. Indeed, the literal meaning of the term is not emperor, but only a king "established at the centre of a circle of kings." King Bharata was a great prince of this order. As a *rajachakravarti*, his political position in the land was not that of the administrative head of any large and centralised government, but only that of the recognised and respected centre and symbol of a confederation of brother princes. This was the general character of all our great princes in the old days. And this being so it is not possible to hold that the unity indicated by the name Bharatavarsha was, in any way, either a political or administrative unity. Neither was it a religious or sacerdotal unity. Unlike Krishna or Buddha, Christ or Mahomed, this Bharata was not the founder or centre of any creed or cult. He was not even the promulgator of any social or sacerdotal code. Indeed, there were in the days when our land first received this name of Bharatavarsha, almost as many sects and schools of religion in this country as there are now. The unity that this name Bharatavarsha indicated, was, thus, not a religious unity either. In the presence of many races and cultures in India even in those early days, convincing evidence of which is supplied by all our old books, it is equally impossible that this unity should have been a mere racial unity. What, then, is the character of the unity which lies at the back of this name Bharatavarsha, by which we have called and known our country from almost the very beginning of our history?

The unity of India was, thus, neither racial nor religious, nor political nor administrative. It was a peculiar type of unity, which may, perhaps, be best described as cultural. Bharata stood before the multitudinous peoples that inhabited the territories that took his name, as representative of a great civilisation and culture. Bharata was, as I have said, a Vedic character. It is not at all likely that at the early period of our history when our continent received this name of Bharatavarsha, the Aryan settlers had actually spread themselves over the whole land. Even at the time of the Mahabharata, there were extensive tracts not yet brought within the control of the Aryans. But still, it can scarcely be doubted that from a much earlier period of the history of this land, the Aryan civilisation had commenced to profoundly influence and visibly dominate it from end to end. And it was as the representative and symbol of this dominating culture, that Bharata gave his name to this great continent, though it was divided then as now into many provinces and principalities; inhabited by many races speaking many dialects, professing many religions, and obeying many different laws and customs.

ARYAN EXPANSION IN INDIA.

What I have called the cultural character of Indian unity, is due partly to the peculiar genius of the Indo-Aryan, and partly to the very peculiar methods by which the Aryan settlers of India spread themselves over the whole of this continent, quietly absorbing all the numerous races and cultures of the land into their own body. These methods are practically unknown in the other parts of the world. The methods of social expansion known to history, in the other parts of the world, are either through religious proseletyzation, or through political conquests, and more often, perhaps, through a combination of the two. Both the Christian and the Moslem communities of the world grew thiswise. It is the common method of social expansion in all credal religions. As we find it in the history of Christianity or Islam, so we find it in the history of Buddhistic expansion also. The mere acceptance of the Buddhist or the Christian or the Moslem creed, makes a person at once a member of the Buddhist, the Christian or the Mahomedan community. This has been one method of social expansion. The other method is political. It is the method of conquest. In this method, sometimes the conquering people spread themselves over the conquered country, and slowly assimilate the conquered races into their own body, or, if the disparity in culture between the two be too wide for such assimilation, the latter are driven out and become gradually extinct as has happened in our own age to the American Indians and the Australian Aborigines. Sometimes it so happens also, as we found in the case of the Norman conquerors of England, that it is the conquered, who, possessed with larger virility, slowly assimilate the conquerors into their own body, and thus develop a new and a composite nation, which, however, gradually attains a practically homogeneous character, especially if the process of assimilation be helped by a common credal religion owned and practised by both the component communities.

The expansion of the Aryan society in India followed neither of these two usual methods known to history. The Aryan religion was never credal. Buddhism is no doubt a credal religin,o and is of Indo-Aryan origin. But though what may be called Buddhist

Imperialism, under the great Asoka, consolidated to a very large extent the fundamental unity of India, Buddhism as a creed had no perceptible influence in this work. In any case, Buddhism did not create the ancient unity of India. The name Bharatavarsha is older than Buddhism, and consequently the unity that was seized by those who gave to our continent this significant historic name, was in no sense a credal. or religious unity. Nor was it a political unity, as I have already said, due to extensive political conquests and the gradual absorption of the conquered peoples by the conquering community. The early Aryan settlers did no doubt at one time fight and conquer the aboriginal races of Northern India. That was a necessity of the situation in which they first found themselves. But the peculiarly peaceful and humanitarian spirit of their culture, soon put a stop to these barbarian methods. The Aryan expansion over the greater part of India, and more particularly among the civilised Dravidian peoples of the South, was effected by other and infinitely more civilised and even spiritual means.

THE NATURE OF THE OLD ARYAN PROPAGANDA.

Hinduism, as the religion of the Indo-Aryan is popularly called, has never been a missionary religion like Buddhism or Christianity or Islam. These so-called missionary religions are credal, and, therefore, can easily propagate themselves by the prevailing missionary method of mere preaching. These missionary religions have a very prominent intellectual emphasis, and are, therefore, essentially instructive in their methods of propagation. Of course every religion has its own special disciplines and constructive spiritual methods. But in the so-called missionary religions, intellectual instructions must precede the real constructive and spiritual disciplines.

In all these credal religions, the acceptance of their special dogmas, is an absolute condition precedent to the initiation into their truly spiritual disciplines, because these latter have always to work upon the former. The acceptance of the Christian dogmas of the Incarnation and the Trinity is absolutely needed for the pursuit of the inner spiritual disciplines of Christianity. In all inner spiritual culture, suggestion and imagination play a very vital part. This suggestion comes in all the credal religions from their particular creeds. These creeds must, therefore, be accepted and fully believed in by those who are to be initiated into the deeper life and culture of these credal religions. In Hinduism, however, owing to its non-credal character, the method has always been predominently constructive. The true Hindu teacher never asks for any declaration of creed from his pupil, nor even imposes his own, or, indeed, any sort of intellectual opinions upon him He does not seek to forcibly shake or destroy the ideas and faiths that the disciple may have imbibed, either from society, or from his parents or previous teachers. Our faiths, he knows, are the result of our inner temperament and outer education and experiences. Real change of faith is, therefore, impossible without a change in this temperament, brought about through long course of psychophysical, intellectual, and ethical disciplines, and the replacement of the old prepossessions by new ones created through a new and different order of experience. When this is done, the legitimate opinions and faiths proper and natural to the disciples' inner intellectual and spiritual state, grow of themselves. Faiths and opinions that grow thuswise have a vitality and truth which no creeds, however natural or healthy these may be, can have, when imposed from the outside through force of supernatural authority or formal logic. What the true Hindu teacher does, even in our own day, for the propagation of his cult or faith, the ancient Aryan settlers of India did for the promulgation of their special culture among the multitudinous peoples of their continent. They propagated their superior culture, not by the popular missionary methods of preaching and proseletyzation, but through the introduction of their socio-ethical arrangements and disciplines among their non-Aryan neighbours. And they did so by the promulgation of their special social economy.

VARNASRAMADHARMA OR THE CASTE-AND-ORDER LAW.

This social économy is summed up by what is called Varnasramadharma (the caste-and-order law) in Sanskrit. The castes are, as you know, four in number. They are :—(i) the Brahmins, (ii) the Ksatriyas, (iii) the Vaisyas, and (iv) the Sudras. The first three castes who alone belonged to the Aryan communion, represent the three great functions of the social organism, namely, (i) the intellectual and the spiritual, (ii) the administrative and the military, and (iii) the economic and the industrial. These are universal social functions. In every society we have people who discharge these three fundamental functions of the social life. The Sudra did not originally belong to the Aryan communion. He was perhaps, originally, either captive of war, who, according to universal ancient custom, was reduced to the status of the domestic or agricultural labourer in the victorious community; or was, possibly, a member of a very low and primitive tribe or race, absolutely unfitted, both intellectually and morally, to undertake any of the first three functions of the social organism in the more advanced Aryan community. This caste-system, more or less universal, in some shape or other, in all old-world civilisations, was, however, joined in India to another, and a supremely significant law and order, known as the asramas, which literally mean stages or stations of life. Society was divided into the above four caste-divisions. Individual life was divided into these four asramas or stations or stages. Distinctions based upon fundamental social functions, however universal and even necessary for the preservation and development of the collective life of society, have an inevitable tendency to breed pride in those who are called upon to discharge the superior functions, and envy in those who have to fill the lower places. Division of social functions, especially in the earlier stages of evolution, when the offices have of necessity to be hereditary,—inevitably leads to these moral evils. These divisions cannot be absolutely eliminated from any form of social organisation, however democratic it may be. And a perplexing problem before every healthy society is how so to adjust the relations between the higher offices of society and the individuals who must fill them, that the enjoyment of these offices shall breed no pride of position in them, nor create the conceit of any superior distance between them and the rest of the communiy. The ancient Indo-Aryans seem to have discovered in this arrangement or order of the asramas or stages, a happy solution of this universal social problem, which even our modern democracies with all their cry of equality and freedom have not yet been able successfully to tackle.

The greatest moral and spiritual danger of the system of caste such as obtained, not only in India, but in almost every ancient society and culture, in some form or other, lies, as I have said, in the almost inevitable pride of office (and later on also of birth owing to the hereditary character of these offices) which it generates in the so-called higher castes. The only true remedy against this evil is to be found in placing the individual members of society under some disciplines as will train their minds to habits of more or less complete self-detachment, and thereby prevent them from identifying their individualities with any high social function or office that they may be called upon to discharge or fill. This was, clearly, the object of this law of stages or asramas that was joined to the caste-laws of the ancient Aryan community of India. The first of these asramas was that of the student or the brahmachari. In this stage every individual was absolutely equal to every other individual, whatever the rank or office, that is the caste, of their parents might be. The brahmachari, in the house of his teacher or guru, could claim no honour in virtue of his birth or heritage, could earn or own no property. and, whether the son of prince or of a common soldier, or of an ordinary artisan, had to beg for his daily food from the public, and perform any service, the meanest not excluded, that his guru might impose upon him.

Here there was absolute equality between one student and another. It was the recognition of the fundamental equality between men *as* men. He was allowed no vacation such as the modern student has, when he might go home to his parents, and resuming, however temporarily, his place as the son of his father, might thus get into any conceit due to his father's position in the general social order and, thereby, neutralise the effect of the superior disciplines of his order. Here, in the guru's house, he was a mere individual, without any rights or privileges, equal to every other individual of the community. The next stage was that of the householder. Having finished his tutelage, which generally lasted from the eighth to either the sixteenth or the twenty-fourth year of his life, and sometimes even to a later period,—he entered this stage. Here he became a regular and recognised member of the social body, vested with all the rights and obligations of his particular station in life, whether as king or warrior, minister or councillor, or priest or teacher, or the producer or seller of commodities. All the inequalities in life came in here, in the householder's stage, and were due entirely to the variety of social functions which different individuals had to discharge. Having thus served society, raised healthy issues, and trained and brought them up in the ways of his caste and position, in the next or third stage, the individual was encouraged to cultivate the spirit of detachment once more, gradually killing the conceits that might have been bred in him by his accidental place and function as a member of society. He now retired from active life, and adopted the duties and disciplines of the higher and the contemplative life. And, finally, if he lived long enough, and was able to attain complete self-detachment, he might enter the fourth or the last of these stages or asramas, that of the sannyasin or the mendicant, when his one aim in life became to absolutely lose all conceit of isolated individuality, and thus identify himself entirely with the universal.

The ancient Aryan social economy was based upon this varnasrama, or caste-and-order scheme. This caste-and-order law sums up the whole soul and spirit of ancient Hindu culture. Through the establishment of this law, the Aryans brought the divergent races and cultures of India within their own fold. And it is here, in this varnasramadharma, that we must look for the secrets of that strange unity which the name Bharatavarsha implied.

And it was comparatively easy for the Indo-Aryan to establish his varnasrama law all over this vast continent, because, at certain stages of social evolution, there exists in every society some arrangement or other that wonderfully falls in with the Hindu's system of castes. At this stage there exist in every community, individuals or families who, either as priests or, in still lower cultures, even as medicinemen, discharge the religious and educational functions of their society, and who, therefore, correspond to the Aryan Brahmins. Similarly there are others who fight and rule, and are, therefore, akin to the Aryan Kshatriyas. And others again, who are devoted to agriculture or handicrafts, and who correspond, thus, to the Vaisyas of the Aryan economy. In every society there exist, at these earlier stages, another class also, who belong to alien tribes and cultures, and being admitted into a dominant and conquering community either as captives of war or in any other way, become mere labourers and slaves. These correspond to the Sudras of the Aryan communion. And owing to this fundamental affinity between the caste-order of the Indo-Aryans and the general social scheme of the non-Aryan communities of India, it became very easy for the former to almost imperceptibly absorb the latter. And they did so by simply putting, so to say, the seal of their own caste-system, upon the already existing social order of their non-Aryan neighbours. This peculiar process of social expansion created absolutely no perceptible disturbance in the communities effected by it. The method was strictly evolutionary, and not revolutionary, as it has generally been in other parts of the world.

But the Hindu system of caste did not stand, as I have already told you, by itself. It was organically bound up with the law of the asramas or stages of life. It is this asrama-law that preserved the humanity of the Hindu in the face of the inequalities created by the system of caste. It was these special disciplines of the asramas which as long as they were faithfully pursued by the so-called higher castes, developed an ideal of spiritual democracy, unknown to the rest of the world;

and it may perhaps be reasonably held that the real cause of the degradations of mediæval Hindu society was not to be found in the system of caste so much, if at all, as in the divorce between the varnas and the asramas, between the outer functions and inequalities of the caste-life, and the inner spiritual ideals and disciplines that were organically connected with these in the earlier periods of our history and culture.

THE ASRAMA-LAW.

The Aryans of India did not only put their own caste-scal upon the natural social divisions of their neighbouring non-Aryan communities, which was an easy enough work, but also brought these new social orders under the law and discipline of the asramas or stages. This was the special contribution of the Aryans of India to the evolution of the non-Aryan communities of the country which they absorbed into themselves.

This is how the general character of these non-Aryan communities was fundamentally changed by what may well be called a strange process of idealisation and spiritualisation. The caste economy gave to these new acquisitions the outer forms of the Aryan social structure : the law and disciplines of the asramas communicated to them the inner spirit of the Aryan culture. The moment these non-Aryan peoples received the badge of the Brahminical social economy and accepted the disciplines of the Brahminical culture, they became, both in form and substance, part and limb of the great Aryan community. The priests of the non-Aryan communities, when adopted into the Aryan fold, became Brahmins not merely in name, but also in fact ; and though preserving all the old peculiarities of their tribal or racial laws and customs, became in every respect the absolute equals of the holiest of the Aryan Brahmins. The same thing happened also in regard to the other castes. The different castes in the different provinces thus fully retained all their old, and even non-Aryan provincialities, after their assimilation by the Aryan community. The Brahmin of Madras or Bombay, therefore, differs in many respects from those of Bengal or Cashmere. Things and usages absolutely prohibited to the Brahmins of one province, are freely permitted to those of another. Often times the personal and civil law of the people, thus brought into the Aryan fold, were allowed to remain in tact. But all these endless diversities notwithstanding, there was absolute social equality between the members of the same caste in the different provinces. As the Aryan society absorbed the different classes of the non-Aryan society, by putting upon them its own caste-order seal, in accordance with their respective places and functions in their old community; so also the gods of these non-Aryan peoples were accepted into the Aryan pantheon, being interpreted according to Aryan ideas and conceptions, while even their special liturgies and worships were also retained, sometimes in their original forms, and sometimes with modifications, but always with a new and spiritual interpretation, for the special use and profit of the newly acquired communities. And when a nation grows in this way, it must necessarily retain almost endless diversities of customs and rituals, faiths and worships, sacraments and disciplines, inside its broad and catholic unity. This is the real psychology of the perplexing diversities of our cults and cultures.

ARYAN METHODS OF UNIFICATION.

But while granting the utmost freedom to the different communities not merely to maintain but even to develop their respective peculiarities, both of thought and institutions, the Aryan nation-builders took great care to ordain certain rules and rituals, certain sacraments and ceremonials, that were binding upon all the sections of the expanding Aryan society, and that sought to preserve and strengthen their fundamental unity. The sacrament of the Upanayana, popularly known as the ceremony through which every boy of the first three castes, called the twice-born castes, is vested with the Brahminical insignia of the so-called sacred thread, is binding on all the Brahmins and Kshatriyas and Vaisyas to whatever province they may belong, and whatever may be their faith or their personal law, or provincial customs. The daily repetition of the Vedic text known as the Gayatri is another obligation of this class. A Brahmin may worship any god he likes, may belong to any sect or denomination, whether old or new, but he must repeat the Gayatri every day. There are local gods and sectarian sanctities, but there are a few gods who receive universal homage, and some places that are sacred to every Hindu of every denomination. And it is significant that these sacred places, visited by devout pilgrims of every sect and from every province, are found very widely spread over the whole Continent. Hurdwar near the source of the Ganges, Prayag (modern Allahabad) and Benares, in Northern India; Gaya in Behar; Nasik in central India; Dvarka in Kathewad; and Kumbhakonam and Rameshvar in Southern India,—are some of these sacred places. Pilgrims from every Indian province are used to visiting these distant places, and thus are able to visualise the unity of their sacred country—their karmabhumi or the land where they have to work for the attainment of merit and the destruction of demerit. And by this means they carry the experiences of different social and religious life of distant parts of the country to their respective homes, to at once broaden their outlook and strengthen the sense of national unity in them. But the most significant formula of national unity invented by the Indo-Aryans is found in the sacred text which every Hindu has to use, whether he be a Brahmin or a non-Brahmin, every time he bathes or sits down to worship his God,—the text for the sacrificial purification of water. It runs thus:—

> Gangeca Jamunecaiva Godavari Sarasvati
>
> Narmmada Sindhu Kaveri jalesmin sannidhin kuru.

And it meaus :—May the Ganges, the Jumna, the Godaveri, the Sarasvati, the Nerbuda, the Indus, and the Kaveri enter into this water. These are the great rivers of the Indian Continent. They cover practically the entire riparian system of this great land. It is along the course of these great rivers, which, in the days before the invention of the railway, were everywhere the highways of commerce and culture, that the sacred stream of Aryan culture flowed over this land. This is why they are so sacred to the Indo-Aryan. And the Hindu wherever he may be in his wide country, by repeating this text during his daily baths and worships, remembers the unity of his country and his people. And all these are very conclusive proof of the fact that at a very early period of our history we had fully realised a very deep, though complex, kind of organic unity at the back of all the apparent diversities and multiplicities of our land and people.

HINDU INDIA.

India was far more than a mere geographical expression or entity, even from the earliest period of Hindu history. You will find ample evidence of it in our great Epics. In fact you find in the Mahabharata itself, the clearest evidence of a very extensive and conscious attempt to work up a great Hindu Confederacy that would unite the whole continent in one powerful and well-ordered federal whole. This was clearly the motif of the Bharata War. Sree Krishna was the divine stage-manager of this great historic drama. He is to a very large extent the *dieu ex machina* of this national plot. And Sree Krishna was, without doubt, the first and the greatest empire-builder that not only India, but the world has as yet known. But the empire that he desired to build up in India was very different from what has been known as such in other parts of the world. It was not to be an empire based upon the subjection of extensive territories and immense populations to a centralised Government represented by a small class or coterie. His was the true ideal of empire. The central aim of the Bharata War which Sree Krishna in some sense himself brought about, was not to acquire territory, but to work out a great socio-political synthesis in India, upon the basis of Dharma, and thus to combine the numerous races and divergent cultures of the continent, into one organic whole. And this ideal of a spiritually-inspired and culturally-combined federation that Sree Krishna had in view in directing the Bharata War, was fairly, if not fully, realised in ancient Hindu history. Buddhistic Imperialism, under Chandragupta and Asoka, whose suzereinty was acknowledged from the confines of Burma on the east, to the very heart of the modern Afghanistan on the west, helped materially to further develop and consolidate this fundamental Indian unity, which had commenced to be worked up from before even the great Bharata War.

MAHOMEDAN INDIA.

India was, thus, a great country, united in a common culture, though divided into many provinces and principalities, possessing a common life, though following diverse laws and customs, and pursuing, through diverse ways, a common spiritual and social ideal,—when the Mahomedans came to us. The Moslem rulers of India came into these invaluable inheritances of the Hindus. And they added new and equally valuable elements to the old national life and consciousness of the country. The old Hindu unity was essentially socio-religious. It was the unity of common spiritual ideals and disciplines. The Mahomedans came, however, with a different culture and a different order of experience to us. The genius of Islam is essentially Semitic. The peculiarity of the Semitic race-consciousness consists in its dominating legalism. Its emphasis is more on the positive than on the imaginative and emotional elements of life. The exquisite emotionalism and idealism of Islam, as found in the art and literature of Persia, is the contribution of the

Aryan race-consciousness to this great world-religion. These elements were native to the soil of India. India had no need of Islam for the deepening of her spiritual or emotional life. What her Moslem rulers did was to add certain positive contents of the national life to her old consciousness and culture. Islamic law and administration helped, through these contributions, to simultaneously deepen and broaden the foundations of our national life and unity. To the old community of socio-religious life and ideals, the Mahomedans now added new elements of administrative and political unity. There were still many more or less independent principalities in the land, but practically all owned at least a kind of nominal allegiance to the Central Government at Delhi. Local and communal laws, as well as denominational customs and rituals still held sway over the people, but all, irrespective of caste or community, became equally subject to certain laws and obligations, known only to Islam. The whole country became subject to one criminal law, the Mahomedan, and to one common judiciary, the Kadi and Kazi. Local imposts and provincial finances practically remained as under the Hindu Administrations, but a wide and general system of imperial revenue and taxation was imposed upon all the country subject to the Central Government at Delhi. As in the hey-day of the Roman Empire, all roads in Europe led, they say, to Rome; so in the hey-day of the Mogul Empire in India, all roads led to Delhi or Agra. The old unity of India and the ancient national life and consciousness of her multitudinous peoples, were thus considerably deepened and enlarged under Moslem rule. The British came into all these glorious inheritances of their predecessors, the Hindus and the Mahomedans of India. They have not had to create any new national consciousness in the country: but have simply been adding fresh elements to the old, old life and unity of the land. India had ceased to be a mere geographical expression or entity long long before the advent of the British East India Company among us. It had been a social unit long long before the Mahomedans came to her with a new cry and culture, to give her something that she lacked and to receive in return from her something that they themselves lacked. The old Indian unity, inspite of local and communal and denominational differences and diversities was still to some extent, not in its details, but in its general outline and outlook, more or less homogenous. It was at any rate what may be called a Hindu unity. This unity had been worked up through the subsumption of just one or two comparatively developed, and numerous nebulous and undeveloped, that is undifferentiated, cultures under one dominating ideal and principle supplied by the Aryan consciousness and culture. The Mahomedans came, however, with a fully developed and world-conquering culture. The necessity of the situation required, therefore, a higher synthesis than what had been previously worked up. Indian unity, always more or less of a federal type, now became still more pronouncedly so. Hinduism, ever ready to accept and accommodate whoever came to her in the name of God and could furnish positive proofs of true spiritual acquisitions, made room now for many a Moslem saint and devotee, in her invisible temple. New Hindu cults, like those associated with the holy names of Nanak and Kabir, came into being in the attempt to work out some sort of a synthesis between Hinduism and Islam. And as the naturally-broad spirit of Hindu culture was further broadened through Moslem contact, so the old Semitic legalism and absolutism of Islam also considerably relaxed its native rigidities through its contact with the spirit of Hindu universalism. Indian

Mahomedanism assumed a form and developed certain characters and tendencies unknown to the rest of the Islamic world. Thus we had, under the Moguls a new India, larger, broader, at once more differentiated and more united a more organic, though not yet fully organised, national life and consciousness than what we had before. The British came to this India: and not to an unorganised, unconscious, and undeveloped chaos, having simply a geographical entity. And in view of all this, it is unpardonable ignorance to say that India was always and still is, a mere geographical expression, and the Indians have always been and still are a chaotic congregation of many peoples, an incoherent and heterogenous collection of tribes and races, families and castes, but not in any sense a nation.

LETTER III.

INDIA: THE MOTHER.

CULTURAL UNITY AND NATIONAL UNITY.

In your last letter you raise the very pertinent question, whether cultural unity is the same as national unity. "Many Europeans," you say, "would not deny that under the Hindus, India had a common culture. So has Europe to-day, But yet Europeans are not one nation. How, then, can the old cultural unity of India prove her national unity also?"

I am glad that you have raised this question. It drew by attention to a thing that I might have, otherwise, overlooked.

I fully admit that the bases of European nationalities are not really a common culture. Of course, the members of the different nations in Europe, as elsewhere, are participators in a common culture, but that culture is not specifically their own, it is not national, but continental. For, culturally, all Europe is one: and even America is not different from Europe in this respect. There are differences of national characteristics, as between the British and the French, or between the Germans and the Russians, or the Italians and the Spaniards. But there is really little or no difference in cultural ideals between them. There is practically one religion, one social economy, one ideal of life and art, one broad culture and civilisation all over Europe and America. Racially also there is practically little difference between one European nation and another. Yet they are not one people, but a group of many distinct peoples, who go by the common name of European. Apparently it is the same in India also. There may be one culture in India, but yet many separate nationalities.

But let us see what really constitutes nationality. We know that Eurore has developed a particular type of nations. In Europe a nation means a group of humans who (i) occupy a common territory; (ii) are subjects of a common state: (iii) generally speak one language: (iv) profess one religion, though there may be sectarian differences: (v) have one common social economy, and (vi) participate in a common culture. These are accepted connotations of nationality in Europe. As I have already said, some of these elements are even common to all the western nations. These are, religion, culture, and social economy. Thus the really distinguishing features of European nationalities are territorial and political unity. The differentiating factors between one nationality and another in Europe are, therefore, not cultural but geographical. Of course some kind of territorial unity is an essential factor of nationality everywhere. As our physical organisation is the fundamental material basis of our personal lives, so territorial unity is to national lives. This fundamental basis of nationality is common to both Europe and Asia. It is a universal factor of national life. The fundamental difference between European nationalism and Indian nationalism lies on the excessive emphasis of the one on territorial and of the other on cultural unity. The emphasis on territorial unity in national differentiations, when it is associated with a general community of religious ideals and social economies between different neighbouring nations, means ultimately an excessive emphasis upon conflicts of mere temporal interests. It is these mean temporal interests that divide the modern European nations from one another. Economic conflicts, industrial competitions, greedy rivalries for the acquisition of unappropriated territories and the possession of unexplored markets, these are what have contributed to the quickening and preservation of nationalism in Europe, and have kept the nations apart from one another. But for these carnal conflicts, Europe might well have been to-day as much a nation, as India was under the Hindus, and what she is essentially even to-day.

THE FEDERAL TYPE OF NATIONALITY.

But the type of nation-hood which Europe would then develop would be different from what exists in Europe at the present time. There is an element of homogeniety in all the European nations at the present time, which is absent in India. This homogeniety is due to the peculiar course of evolution which these nations have passed through. In the earliest stages of social evolution, nations grow through the accretion of more or less fluid tribal organisations: and owing to this fluidity, the tribal fusion becomes easy, and the resulting nation absolutely homogenous in all respects.

This was the general process of nation-building in ancient Europe. So also it must have been in the earliest stages of the evolution of the Aryan community in India. The original Aryan type was also completely homogenous, like all the older types of nations. When, even, at a somewhat later stage of social evolution, different nebulous tribes combine to form one larger tribe or a nation, under the influence of some one particular and comparatively more developed tribe or culture, they gradually adopt the language, the religion, the social ideal and economy of this dominating community. It is thus that there grows a kind of homogeniety even in these new social units also. This is really the cause of the homogeniety of those European nations that are racially heterogenous. But at a later stage of social evolution when not fluid tribal cultures, but advanced and developed nations, first come into contact and conflict with one another, and then, in course of time, under pressure of new historic forces, combine to form one united nation, this early homogenous character can hardly be maintained.

Owing, however, to the peculiar conditions of social evolution in Europe, since the break up of the Roman Empire, the old homogenous character of nationality was not seriously disturbed even when comparatively advanced tribes combined to form national units. Europe had been already Christianised. Christianity meant not merely a common religious creed, but also a common social ideal. It is not merely a creed but essentially a culture. And owing to this fact, the fusion of even advanced communities did not violently destroy the old homogenous character of nationhood. But still there are many heterogenous elements even in the most consolidated nationalities of Europe. The British people, for instance, are by no means homogenous. The British are a composite nation: the component entities being English, Welsh, and Scotch. England has, no doubt, tried her utmost for many centuries past, to crush out the independent national consciousness of both Wales, and Scotland. But has she completely succeeded in her attempt? She imposed her own language upon these two peoples, thus practically killing the old Gaelic and Celtic languages and literatures. But all these repre- sions notwithstending, the national conciousness of neither Wales nor Scotland has been entirely killed. The cry to-day in both these countries, as you know better than I do,—is for an independent national existence, inside a true Federation of the British Empire. What both Wales and Scotland, and even Ireland, desire is not simply political self-government, but rather a self-contained and self-controlled national life, which will give them free scope for the development of those mental and moral and spritual characteristics in which these peoples stand differentiated from others; and thereby enable them to make their special contribution to the general life and culture of Universal Humanity. The Home Rule propaganda, as you know, does not mean a demand for national isolation, but rather for a healthy inter-national federation. And it indicates the nature of the coming type of social evolution.

THE OLD INDIAN TYPE, EEDERAL.

India, my child, had developed this federal type of nationality ages and ages ago. In Christendom, this federal idea is of very recent growth. It was first applied to the organisation of the United States of America. But even this application was only to one part of the social life, namely, the organisation of the State. The political constitution of America is alone federal. But India had developed a much wider and fuller type of federalism. Our religion, as I have already told you, has been organised after the federal ideal. Hinduism is not one uniform religious culture, nor based upon one universal creed or one particular system of dogmas, like Christianity or Islam, or Buddhism; but it is a group of many diverse theologies and dogmas and disciplines and rituals and worships, all moved, however, by one common spirit and pursuing one common ideal. Our social economy has similarly been of a distinct federal character. The Hindu Society is really a group of many communities, each practically independent of the others and autonomous within its own sectional or communal or caste life, but combined with the others in the pursuit of a common ideal, namely, the revelation of God in Man. Our States were also of this federal type. Each Village Community was autonomous within the limits of the communal life and concerns of the village, but formed part of the larger life of the province or principality. And sometimes even these provinces and principalities combined to form large confederacies, which, while leaving all local autonomies absolutely in tact, combined them into one great organic whole, for the pursuit of larger ends and the realisation of more general purposes. This is really the advanced type of social organisation towards which humanity is slowly moving. In fact, India furnishes a model of that Universal Federation, the Federation of the World, which is the dream of the seers and prophets of modern Western humanity.

CHARACTERISTICS OF WESTERN PATRIOTISM.

And all these peculiarities of our history and evolution, have helped to develop a type of patriotism among us which is almost unknown in Europe. Owing to the fudamental unity of the religion and culture of Europe, the different nations of your great Continent are separated from one another by considerations of mere material interests. And when the carnal conflicts of mean material interests divide one people from another, and supply the motif of their nationality and patriotism, the national character developes all those traits with which we are familiar in Europe. In the first place, patriotism evoked by the conflicts of mere material interests, naturally becomes much keener and stronger than when its appeal lies to man's higher instincts and ideals. Constituted as man is, his passion for material advantages and possessions is, naturally, much stronger than for things moral or spiritual. And owing to the predominant secular reference of his national life and competitions, the European's passion for his country has always been much stronger than what we have ever known in India. On the other hand, patriotism inspired by considerations of material gain and brought into play through conflicts of mean secular interests, must inevitably become narrow and selfish, intolerent and aggressive. This is, to a very large extent, the general character of patriotism in Europe. It is this secular patriotism that drives the great nations of Europe to so perpetually "snarl at each other's heels." And it is for this very reason also that in Europe, love of the Fatherland has not yet visibly broadened into any real love of Humanity. This type of narrow, selfish and, pathological patriotism was never developed in ancient India.

THE HINDU IDEAL OF PATREOTISM.

Our highest ideal of love and devotion to our country is to be found in our conception of our land as Mother. On the face of it, the conception is not peculiar to India. Other peoples have also addressed their land in the terms of the parental relation. The ancient

Romans called their country, patria or the fatherland. Germany is in our day addressed as the Fatherland by the Germans. We too have the expression motherland among us, जननी जन्म भूमिश्च स्वर्गादपि गरीयसी । "The mother and the mother-land are greater than heaven itself," says a Sanskrit text. I cannot tell you just now whether the expression janma-bhumi or motherland is a modern or an ancient usage in Sanskrit. The text I have quoted is, however, undoubtedly very modern. But even if we had the term motherland in our ancient language and literature, it was not the highest expression of our ideal of what is known as patriotism in Europe.

Expressions like fatherland or motherland are clearly metaphorical. There is an element of poetical imagination behind them. The imagination that clothed our conception of our country was, however, of a much superior order. It was not poetical but essentially religious. We addressed our land not merely as janani janmabhumi or mother-country, but simply as Mother. I do not know of any other people who ever did so.

MOTHER AND MOTHERLAND.

The real concept Mother as applied to India by her children has no metaphor behind it. Of course most of our modern-educated people use and understand the word in a poetical and metaphorical sense. But this is because their education and environment have more or less completely divorced their thought and imagination from the ancient realities of their language and literature. There are, indeed, numerous words in common use among us to-day, that have entirely lost their original sense, owing to the loss of the genuine thought-life of the people in the wilderness of un-understood and unassimilated foreign words and concepts accumulated by our present system of education. When, for instance, we talk of Dharma we do not understand it to mean either law of being or sacrifices and rituals or duty, the three different senses in which the word was always used among us, but the imported concept religion. Similarly, we use the word Nitee, which really means strategy and statecraft, for European morals. With the Europeanisation of our mind and modes of thinking even our words have been perceptibly Europeanised. It is not at all surprising, therefore, that the original significance of the word Mother as applied to our country, has also been largely lost to many of our educated countrymen, who see nothing more sacred or serious in it than a very tender and beautiful metaphor.

It was, however, very different with those who first applied this word to their land. The Mother in what people call the motherland, was to them not a mere idea or fancy, but a distinct personality. The woman who bore them and nursed them, and brought them up with her own life and substance was no more real a personality in their thought and idea than the land which bore and reared, and gave food and shelter to all their race. But to seize the full truth and reality of this concept you will have to study it in the light of the entire Nature Philosophy of the Hindus.

THE NATURE GODS OF THE HINDUS.

Nature to the Hindu was never absolutely inanimate or impersonal. But when I say this, do not rush to the easy and convenient conclusion that it is only an example of what the Europeans call animism, and is therefore something which is common to primitive culture. Indeed, personally, I strongly object to the application of this term animism to even the lowest forms of human faiths or religions.

The very conception is crude and absolutely empirical. Animism means really the ascription of life to non-life. Faiths that project or posit distinct personalities behind natural or material objects and phenomena are classed as animistic by European thinkers. But has Europe discovered all the secrets of Nature ? Can she draw the line between life and non-life ? Has she been able, my child, to remove the mask of that which her children, with all the inordinate conceits of innocent childhood, so glibly talk of as "personality ?" Has our much-vaunted scientific culture been able to even suggest a solution of the unfathomable mysteries of this personality ? On the contrary, are not all your highest Theistic Thinkers and Christian Divines practically doing the same thing which they treat with such superior contempt in those whom they call savage and superstitious ? Do they not themselves posit a Mind, an Intelligence, a Spirit, a

God, behind all the inanimities of what they write down as Nature, with a capital N ? And is there any fundamental difference in kind between the animistic explanation of natural phenomena, familiar to what is called primitive culture, and the theistic explanation offered by the modern thinker and theologian? Both belong to the same class. Both posit life and intelligence and emotion and will, which really means a personality, at the back of natural phenomena that are apparently lifeless, unconscious, and incapable of emotion or volition. The difference between them lies in this only, namely, that while the so-called primitive man posits numerous agencies behind phenomena, the modern Christian thinker posits not many, but One Agent behind these. And it is exceedingly doubtful whether the modern Christian explanation is more satisfactory than the old heathen explanations.

The Hindu has, from of old, posited

individul entities behind different prominent and active natural objects. The sun, the moon, the earth, the sky, the winds, the phenomena of the morning and the evening twilight, the great mountains of his land, as well as all the great rivers along the course of which the stream of his national life and culture flowed from one part of the country to another,—all these had, in his thought, distinct personal entities behind them. Whether it be real or merely imaginary, the popular belief in these personalities behind natural objects and phenomena, was by no means animistic. The natural objects were never looked upon as gods. As there is a distinct difference between our own bodies and what we call our soul, which is the essence and substance of our personalities; so there is a distinct difference between the sun-god or the moon-god, or the earth-god, etc., and the natural objects with which these are visibly associated. Having from almost prehistoric times, reached the supreme spiritual consciousness of the separation of the soul from the body in the human kingdom, the Hindu found absolutely no difficulty in accepting the presence of these different divinities in different natural objects,—divinities that are as much invisible and spiritual as the soul of man. The outer objects are not really the gods, but only their bodies, just as our own bodies are not ourselves, but only our outer habiliments. And as the existence of innumerable human personalities does not destroy the Unity of the Supreme, so even the extension of the idea of similar personalities to what is called the natural order of creation, in no way destroys the Divine Unity. In fact the Hindu's belief in gods and goddesses no more makes his religion polytheistic than the Catholic Christian's belief in angels makes Catholicism polytheistic, or the Protestant faith in the Father, the Son, and the Holy Ghost makes Trinitarian Christianity tri-theistic.

HINDU THEORY OF ULTIMATE REALITY.

The origin of the concept Mother as applied by the Hindu to his geographical habitat must be traced, I think, to the ancient Vedic conception of the Earth-God. Subsequent speculations, instead of dissipating, rather on the contrary helped very materially to deepen and vivify, this old idealism. The highest philosophical speculations of the Hindus have posited two ultimate principles, or, more correctly speaking, two final personalities in the universe: one is called Purusha, the other Prakriti. In some shape or other, in one name or another, these dual principles are found in every Hindu system, except perhaps in that of the avowedly materialistic and atheistic schools of the Lokayatas, who had very close affinity with the Epicurians of Greece. The names Purusha and Prakriti belong specifically to the Sankhya system. At the final analysis, two ultimate principles are found in creation, one is the principle of permanence, the other of change. No rational interpretation of cosmic evolution is possible except upon the hypothesis of these two fundamental principles. All evolution means change in some thing which retains its identify through all changes. Like shine and shade, permanence and change always go together: the one is unthinkable and impossible without the other. In our Sankhya system of philosophy, Purusha represents the principle of permanence, and Prakriti that of change. In the Vedantic Philosophy, Purusha is called Isvara and Prakriti Maya: the former representing the noumenal and thc latter the phenomenal aspect of Reality. In the system of the Vaishnavas, Sree Krishna is Purusha and Prakriti is Radha. In the thought of the Shaivaites, Purusha is Shiva and Prakriti is Shakti. The conception of

Mother associated with our geographical habitat is filiated to this old, old, universal Hindu conception of Prakriti: but of Prakriti conceived especially as Shakti.

CHRISTIAN TRINITY AND HINDU PURUSHA-PRAKRITI.

The same necessity of thought that developed the dogma or mystery of the Holy Trinity, gave rise among us to this dogma or mystery of the Purusha and Prakriti. If the Ultimate Reality be, as is admitted in every Theistic system, Intelligent and Self-Conscious, then it must have all the necessary elements of consciousness. Reason or consciousness can work only through duality. Rational or thought life is inconceivable and impossible, without something to know or think of. This something must not be absolutely different from us, nor must it be absolutely identical with us. For we can never know that which we are not: all knowledge is, therefore, really self-knowledge. Nor can we know anything which is not differentiated from us. The object of our knowledge must be the same as ourselves, yet at the same time different from us. And in every act of knowledge or thought we first create, so to say, a separation between ourselves and our object, and immediately this is done, we cancel it again. To quote a well-known saying of one of your own Epropean philosophers, in every act of knowledge or reason, "the self separates itself from itself to return to itself to be itself." And if this be the logic of rational life, and if the Ultimate Reality, by whatever name called, whether God, or Allah, or Brahman, or Isvara, be intelligent and self-conscious, then you must posit in the very Being of that Reality an element of differentiation which, without cancelling the Divine Unity, supplies the object of Divine thought, through which the Divine realises

His own consciousness. The Ultimate Reality being infinite, the object through which that Reality can realise its infinite reason, must also be infinite. As it is true of the rational, so also is it true of the emotional and the volitional life. Love also demands with a view to realise itself an object not different from, yet not absolutely identified with, the lover. This is true also of our will or volition. In all the three elements of the rational or spiritual life, the same process of the separation of the self from itself and its return to itself, with a view to realise itself, is perpetually present. In all these there is a necessary element of differentiation. In all these our object is both different from, yet identical with us. And if you can grasp this fact, my child, you will find absolutely no difficulty in understanding either the truth of the Christian Trinity or our own Mystery of the Purusha and Prakriti.

CHRIST AND PRAKRITI.

That through which the Divine realises Himself in His Own Being is called Christ by the Christians, and Prakriti by the Hindus. This, however, is not the historical Christ, but the Christ of the Trinity, in and through Whom the Father eternally realises His Reason, His Love and His Will or Volition. The process by which the Father eternally separates Himself from Himself and returns to Himself to be Himself, is called, in Christian theology, the Eternal Generation of Christ. It is also described as the Eternal Colloquy between the Father and the Son. All these things are more or less familiar to you. And if you study our own philosophy of the Purusha and Prakriti in the light of these Christian experiences, you will at once seize its profound truth and significance, and per chance also be confirmed in the conviction of the fundamental truth of both the highest Hindu and Christian consciousness. Our Purusha stands for the Father of the Christian Trinity. Our Prakriti stands for the Son of Christian experience. As the Father and the Son are both one yet not one, so are also our Purusha and Prakriti. As the Father realises His Reason and His Love and His Will through the Son, so does Purusha in our thought through Prakriti. As the Son is the prototype of the world, and especially of Humanity, as by Him have all things been made, so our Prakriti is the Regulative Idea of the universe and all things are made by Her. Prakriti is both the efficient and the material cause of the cosmos. What is called the Eternal Generation of Christ, in Christian experience, is called Nitya Leela or the Eternal Sport of the Lord in our literature. The truth is the same, though expressed differently, through different sets of symbols.

The special symbol of the Christian consciousness is filial, that of the Hindu consciousness is nuptial. The Sankhya doctrine of Prakriti, the Vedantic doctrine of Maya, the Vaishnavic conception of Radha, the Shaivaite conception of Shakti,—all these represent the self-same attempt of the human mind and spirit to reach and realise the Mystery of Divine Being, which the Hebrew doctrine of Sophia, the Greek doctrine of the Logos and the Christian doctrine of the Son or Christ, sought to unveil. The ultimate rational explanation of experience has been sought by all these ancient peoples, Hindu, Hebrew, Greek, and the Christians at a later period, in this supreme Divine Mystery.

PRAKRITI AS MAYA, RADHA, AND SHAKTI.

But though there is a fundamental unity between the general conception and philosophy of Prakriti, there are certain marked differences between

Maya, Radha, and Shakti. Prakriti when sought to be seized through the logic of what may be called pure reason, is seen in its aspect of Maya. This Maya is not Illusion, as is popularly interpreted by many European scholars. Even Samkara, the father of the school of Absolute Monism in India, who is popularly cited as an authority in regard to this illusory interpretation of the phenomenal world, ignorantly ascribed to the Vedantic School of Hindu thought,—posited Maya as an element in the Being of Brahman or the Absolute. When questioned by an opponent as to "what was, before creation, the object of the knowledge of Brahman?" Samkara replied:—"It is name and form, the indescribable entity (called Maya), which is neither different from, nor identical with Brahman: this we shall say." And from this it is clear that Maya is Prakriti as conceived in relation to the Reason of God. Radha is the

HARA-GAURI.

same Prakriti conceived, however, not as a necessity of Reason, but of Love and the Emotions. The Vaishnavas describe Radha as the Body of the Emotions of the Supreme, through which the Purusha realises his Love. Radha is Premamayee, or made of Love. She is both the Soul and Satisfaction of Supreme Love. Shakti, on the other hand, is not the Soul of Love, but that of the Divine Will. The Hindu never calls her Premamayee, but only Ichhamayee, not the symbol and instrument of Divine Love but of Divine Will. Maya is, thus, the explanation of our rational experience: Radha of our emotional experience: Shakti of our volitional experience. And the specific function of the will is to work out what the reason or the emotions demand or desire. Reason reveals the truth of things. The emotions enjoy them. The will works to develop and perfect them. The Will of the Supreme lies, therefore, at the back of both cosmic and human evolution. Shakti, as the Soul of the Divine Will, is Energy in cosmic life and evolution. It is what may perhaps be called the Conscience in the inner life of individual humans, the dynamic element in our ethical consciousness. It is Providence in history. In a word, it is that which works out different changes through which the universe is evolving itself. It is Raciality in the history and evolution of races. It is the Spirit of Nationality in national life and evolution.

THE PROBLEM OF PERSONALITY.

The Christ of the Christian Trinity is not a mere Idea, but a Person. It is through the personality of Christ that the Father realises His Own Personality. Dismiss the personality of the Son, and the personality of the Father also vanishes. Or if it is still retained, it is reduced to the objectivity of the Hebrew Godhead. The Personal

God of the New Testament is impossible without the personality of Christ. Like Christ in Christian consciousness, both Radha and Shakti in Hindu consciousness are not mere ideas, but persons. It is through the personality of Radha that Krishna realises His Own Personality. It is through the personality of the same Prakriti, but viewed not through the emotions, but through the will, and called Shakti, that the Personality of Isvara or Shiva is realised. Krishna and Shiva are really one: the two names representing not two entities, but only two aspects of the one and the same Truth or Being. So are Radha and Shakti really One: the two names symbolising not two Beings but one Truth and Reality, viewed from two different stand-points. Brahman represents the Ultimate Reality, in its undifferentiated and therefore impersonal aspect. Krishna represents the same Ultimate Reality, but eternally self-differentiated and, therefore, the fuller truth. Krishna is the Perfected Personality of the Absolute. In Krishna, therefore, as the Hindu Vaishnavas contend, we have a truer and fuller view of the Reality than what we get in the Brahman of the Upanishads. And Krishna of the Vaishnavas is really the same as the Shiva of the Shaivaites, only viewed in another aspect. This is the Shiva of the Shivajnanabodhinee School. And Shakti, as conceived by them, is no more an idea or abstraction than is the Radha of the Vaishnava or the Christ of the Christian.

PRAKRITI AND LOGOS.

The Hindu's conception of Prakriti is thus as much indicative of personality as is the Christian's conception of the Logos. Both Radha and Shakti, the one representing the emotional and the other the volitional aspect of the eternal self-differentiation of the

Absolute, are personalities in the Being of the Deity, just as Christ is in Christian Dogma. But Radha, representing the emotional aspect of Prakriti, has one form only, though quite an infinity of moods. Shakti, however, has many forms. This multiformness is the essential character of the Will. The Will assumes a different form in working out different purposes. And one of these many forms of Shakti is what we call the Spirit of Nationality.

THE BEING BEHIND NATIONALITY.

Nationality, as you may remember, has been defined by Mazzini as the "individuality of peoples." The concept individuality involves being or personality. Mazzini spoke of Humanity as a Being. And judging from this it seems to me that Mazzini conceived Nationality also as a Being. A Being is a self-conscious intelligence that seeks to realise itself through due regulation of means to end. And if there be any intelligence behind national histories and evolutions, if historical movements be not a mere play of blind chance, if, that is, there is any law and purpose behind human history, then it is only natural to conceive a Personality behind national evolutions. In any case, the Hindu did conceive such a Personality behind his own history and evolution, and it is this Personality which he addressed as Mother in his motherland.

And he found little or no difficulty in conceiving such a personality behind his historic evolution, because he had a much clearer grasp of the concept personality than many other peoples. Literally, as you know, persona means a mask; and personality really means something that is masked. Difference of personalities does not, therefore, necessarily imply separate entities but only different appearances. The Christian also holds this belief in regard to the Dogma of the Trinity. The three *Persons* of the Holy Trinity are only different in hypostatis or appearance but one in ousia or essence. Owing to the predominantly monistic emphasis of Hindu thought, the Hindu can more easily understand the truth of the Christian position that different personalities do not break up the fundamental unity of Being than even many orthodox and bigotted Christians. The personality of the Mother in his motherland, therefore, does not in any way destroy, in his thought, the fundamental Unity of Prakriti, any more than the Personality of Prakriti herself destroys the Divine Unity. Prakriti has many forms: and in every form she is a person.

THE PRIMAL FORM OF THE MOTHER.

The first and primal form of the Mother is, therefore, in the very bosom of the Supreme. That is her eternal place and being. In Hindu symbolism, she is seated, in this form, on the lap of Narayana or Mahavishnu. Mahavishnu represents the first step, so to say, in the process of the eternal self-differentiation of the Absolute,—within His Own Being. Here the Mother is undifferentiated Prakriti. She is both Radha and Shakti. Here she is not our Mother as differentiated from your Mother, but the Mother of all that is to be. Here the Mother is the Mother of the unborn Universe. The Spirit of Cosmic Evolution, both human and non-human.

SHAKTI AS JAGADDHATREE.

It is from here, the bosom of her Lord, that Shakti starts upon her manifold functions of cosmic and social evolution. She is the Force that stands behind the evolution of the universe, working out the infinite changes through which the Absolute is progressively realising Himself in the cosmic process. As the Spirit of Race, she

Jagadhatri

stands behind, and directs and controls all racial and social evolution. Her first manifestation here is in the earliest jungle-clearing stage, when man, but scarcely removed as yet from the surrounding animal creation, is engaged in a life-and-death struggle with both his physical and animal environment, to secure a slice of mother-earth for his humble habitation. The Race-Spirit, or Shakti, manifests herself at this stage as a tremendous and relentless animal force, fighting and subjugating the malicious brute forces about her. The Hindu has symbolised her, at this stage, by the figure of the Goddess Jagaddhatree. You have simply to glance at the figure of Jagaddhatree to realise this fact. Jagaddhatree rides a lion. And the lion here is symbolic of the highest animal strength and intelligence. The lion represents not merely a very superior kind of brute force, but its special characteristic is the superior combination of animal strength with animal intelligence. The lion here does not simply stand under Jagaddhatree, but has its fore paw upon a vanquished elephant. The elephant has preserved to us the type of the extinct mammoth. It is a reminder of the mammoth age of terrestrial history and evolution. The mammoth age was characterised by the almost complete domination of the animals over man. Man was then only a weaker animal. Evolution of man, at this stage, worked itself out almost completely through the conflict of the brute in man with the brute in his fearful animal surroundings.

In Shakti, as symbolised by Jagaddhatree, there is apparently no reference to tribal conflicts. The setting of Jagaddhatree is not in human habitations, but rather in wild mountain scenery, where Nature reigns in all her terrific luxuriance, amidst yet more terrific animal life and activities.

Signs of murderous struggle are there, but it is the struggle with animals and not yet with men.

SHAKTI AS KALEE.

The next stage of racial or social evolution is marked by fierce tribal conflicts. Man has, by this time, partially conquered a portion of the earth from the animals, and has made it fit for his habitation. The struggle with wild nature and wilder animals is to a very large extent over. Now the main emphasis is not on his competitions with wild animals, or with the fatal luxuriance of the vegetable kingdom, but rather with brother man. This is the stage of tribal conflicts. And Shakti or the Spirit of Raciality or Nationality as revealed at this stage is symbolised by the Hindu Goddess Kalee. Here we have the clearest symbolisation of a pure human conflict; but the conflict is on the purely animal plane. Kalee rides on no animal. She is without any adornments except the dripping heads of men whom she has herself killed. Her setting is in the heart of the bloody desolations of war. She is dark with anger, and unconscious of the terrible carnage in which she is engaged. Yet, even at this stage of universal war and carnage, the Hindu could not absolutely lose his innate sense of the spiritual and the universal, or his consciousness of the fact that even all this cruelty and carnage notwithstanding, there is Goodness and Love in creation. The aim and objective of evolution, whatever may be its passing and apparent phases, is not to kill but to save, not to destroy but to develop, this principle of Love and Goodness in the world. So Kalee, this fearful Goddess, revelling in carnage, adorned with the skulls of the killed, covered with blood, darkened by all the passions of a competing, quarrelling, fighting, killing humanity,—is still standing on Shiva or the Good. But Shiva lies prostrate at her feet!

A popular Hindu story says that when Kalee was engaged in this work of destruction, she so completely forgot herself that she did not stop with the killing and conquest of her enemies, but threatened, in her passion for war and carnage, to work universal ruin. And it was then that Shiva, the symbol of the Good, who alone in all the worlds could stand the passion of the dread Goddess, threw himself down at her feet, and thus brought her back to herself. Kalee, therefore, stands, naked, and fearful, drunk with the lust of war and blood, on the prostrate form of Shiva, her Lord and Lover.

SHAKTI AS DURGA.

But this is not the final stage of racial or national evolution. The conflicts between the barbaric tribalities, yet but scarcely removed from the animal kingdom, is succeeded by the more organised but, therefore, none the less severe conflicts, between more advanced nations. Here the conflict is between competing colours and rival cultures. Here the Mother is revealed not merely in the animal life and activities of humanity, but in the far more developed and organised national or social organisms. This is the stage when the Hindu symbolised the Mother or Shakti in the form of Durga, popularly called the Tenhanded Goddess. The spirit of Nationality is here fully developed. The social life is completely organised, social functions are clearly differentiated. The rational autonomy of the different departments of life,—military, economic, æsthetic, spiritual, has been fairly established. Yet all these are united in and subordinated to the Unity of the National and the Social Life. Durga represents this perfected type of nationhood. She is the Soul of National Life and Unity. With her ten hands, she joins all the ten points of the compass in her, symbolising the territorial unity of the

DURGA.

Nation's Body. Nay more, her ten hands symbolise also the unity of the whole globe. They are symbols of general terrestrial interrelations and unity. She too, like Jagaddhatree, rides a lion. It shows that the Spirit of the Nation is related vitally and organically to the animal kingdom about her. But they are no longer, as in the early jungle-clearing stage, her enemies and competitors for the possession of mother-earth, but her help and instruments. Brute force is not eliminated, but has been absolutely brought under control. The lion is here the willing slave of the Mother, rendering not sullen but joyous service unto Her, not fearing, but loving her with all the love of his royal nature. But unlike both Jagaddhatree and Kalee, Durga does not stand simply by herself. That was the Mother's form in the earlier undifferentiated stages of social and national evolution. Jagaddhatree and Kalee represent those earlier stages. As symbolising a much more advanced and developed, that is, at once more differentiated and more united, national life,—Durga is supported on one side by Lakshmee, the goddess of wealth, the symbol and spirit of the economic and industrial life and activities of the nation, on the other side, by Sarasvatee, the goddess of learning and the arts, the symbol and spirit of intellectual and æsthetic life and activities. But the economic, the æsthetic and the intellectual activities of any people do not sum up and exhaust the whole range of their social functions and life. The economic activities bring them into almost perpetual conflicts with their neighbouring nations. These conflicts arose in the earliest stages of social evolution, from the competitions and rivalries of neighbouring tribes for territorial expansion and possession. In subsequent stages these arise through industrial competitions between one nation and another. And these conflicts require, for the protection of the economic life and freedom of the people, another department of national activities, namely, the military. It is the national army that up till now has everywhere protected the basal economic life and organisation of every nation. Lakshmee or the Goddess of Wealth or earthly possessions, both in territory and merchandise, has therefore always to be duly protected by Kartikeya or the God of War. If Lakshmee represents the economic life of the nation, Kartikeya represents its military life. Both are equally necessary to a healthy and self-contained national existence. On the other hand, the æsthetic and intellectual life of every nation also requires for its preservation and healthy evolution the spirit of true wisdom as its guide and guru. Science and art, without the spirit of wisdom or universal culture, become abortive and barren. They fail absolutely of their high and lofty purposes, unless guided and controlled by wisdom. Where "knowledge comes, but wisdom lingers," there the inevitable result is the loss of intellectual vigour and spiritual vision. There science becomes charlatanism, and the arts sensual and vicious. In the perfected life of the nation, the ideal that is sought to be symbolised by our Goddess Durga,—the economic life must be protected by the legitimate strength of the arm, and the intellectual and æsthetic life must be guided and controlled, uplifted and spiritualised, by the spirit of the highest wisdom. Ganapati, the so called Elephant-God, who stands next to Sarasvatee in the group of figures representing Durga, represents this Spirit of Wisdom. This is why Durga, with all these, who are one with her, her own progeny and family, has always symbolised the fully realised national life and consciousness in the religious imagination and symbolism of the Hindus. Durga is a form of Prakriti, like Jagaddhatree or Kalee.

While these two represent, however, the Spirit of National Life and Evolution at the first two stages, Durga represents the same Spirit at the last and fully evolved stage of that life.

THE NATIONALIST INTERPRETATION OF DURGA.

These are the many symbols through which we have been worshipping the Mother for countless centuries. It is a strange symbolism, at once both cosmic and social, both national and humanitarian. The Mother whom we worship as Jagaddhatree, or Kalee, or Durga,—and she has many other names also, the great Mahratta nation-builder, Shivaji worshipped her as Bhavanee,—is, however, no mere racial symbol or deity. There is a mysterious combination of the particular and the universal in this, as in almost every other, symbolism of the Hindu religion. It is, therefore, that it appeals to all classes of our people, and is suited to the temperament, culture, and character 'both intellectual and spiritual' of almost all men. The modern multitudes in India do not, perhaps, fully realise the profound nationalist reference of these cults. They look upon Jagaddhatree, Kalee, Durga, and all the other gods and goddesses of popular worship, as forms of the Deity, the Author and Governor of the Universe. To them Jagaddhatree, Kalee, Durga, Bhavanee, and the other gods and goddesses associated with the cult of Shiva and Shaktee, as well as those associated with the cult of Vishnu and Radha, are all simply manifestations of the Lord and Protector of the universe. But the multitudes everywhere do the same. It is only the few in all countries and in every religion, who are able to rise to a full consciousness of the inner meaning and significance of the current dogmas and symbols of their religion. And the deeper meaning of no religion should be sought for in the automatic practices and the traditional and unconscious faiths of its votaries. It is the same with Hinduism as it is with Christianity or Islam or any other religion.

How many among those who not only profess but even teach and preach Christianity, have any understanding or appreciation of the meaning of the Christian Dogmas of the Incarnation and the Trinity? The masses attend the church, accept the sacraments, repeat the prayers, and try, so far as may be, to follow the Ten Commandments, even if they do as much,—and think that their religious duty is fairly discharged. It is the same with my people also. The multitudes observe the outer forms of their religion, but do not understand, and hardly ever care either to enter into, the deeper meaning of what they say or do. It is in the saints and sages, it is in the general course of the historical development of the dogmas and symbols of every religion, in the progressive exegesis and interpretations of these in the light of expanding and deepening spiritual experience, that the true meaning and significance of these dogmas and symbols must be looked for and seized. It is the Christian Fathers to whom one must go for a true interpretation of the Christian mysteries, and not to the Catechist or the Colporteur. It is in the history of the Christian Doctrine that you must seek for its rational meaning and purpose. So also in regard to our own mysteries and dogmas and doctrines. The true meaning of the Cult of the Mother, as I have been trying to explain to you, must be sought for in the course of the historic evolution of it, as well as in the meaning discovered by saints and devotees in their inner spiritual experiences, and not in the extraneous and blind criticisms of the outsider who can, at his best, apply only either the canons of formal logic and the lower intellect, or the generalisations of his own particular spiritual experience, for unlocking them.

THE HISTORY OF THE DURGA CULT.

And if we look into the history or tradition of the Durga Cult, we at once see its profound racial or national reference. According to the Hindu legends, Suratha was the first to inaugurate the worship of Durga. Ask the most illiterate Hindu in the most backward village of Bengal, as to how Durga came to be worshipped, and he will mention the name of Suratha as the first worshipper of Durga. Suratha belonged to the early Satya-Yuga or Golden Age. His was the regular worship. But the current worship of Durga was started by Rama, the hero of the Ramayana. And Durga was worshipped by him ages after Suratha, not at the time appointed by the latter, but at a different time, and so rather irregularly, during a serious crisis in the progress of his war with Ravana, which forms the theme of the Ramayana. The story of the Ramayana clearly refers to a very vital conflict between the Aryan culture of the North and the non-Aryan culture of the South of India. And it was during this vital conflict that the Mother was awakened untimely, to help and save her people. And all these are, it seems to me, ample justification for the nationalist interpretation of the Durga Cult. This interpretation is further confirmed by the whole story of the portion known as Chandee in the Markandeya Purana. This story describes a great conflict between the Devas and the Asuras. The Devas were the representatives and protectors of Aryan culture. The Asuras evidently represented a different and opposing culture and community. It was during this struggle that the Devas created Chandee, one of the manifestations of Durga, out of their combined strength and merit, each of the Devas giving a portion of his own soul and strength for the purpose. She was, thus, the product of the collective life and strength of the godly community. In other words, Chandee was the manifestation of the Spirit of the Hierarchy of the Gods. And when we consider all these, the conclusions presented here regarding the inner meaning and significance of the Durga Cult and the whole range of symbolism associated with it, seems irresistible.

But though there seems to be little doubt that the original meaning of the Durga Cult was essentially racial or national, it soon became, as everything did in the consciousness of the Hindu, universalised. The Mother of the Race or Nation soon became the Mother of Humanity. The Presiding Deity of the Race and Nation became identified with the Lord and Author of the Universe. So Jagaddhatree, Kalee, Durga, and all other names and symbols of Shakti, came to be addressed as Jagatmata or the World-Mother. They became the Mother of All. And this universalisation helped considerably to weaken the old and original significance of the Shakti Cult as what may be called the Cult of Nationality or Patriotism in India.

THE NEW PATRIOTISM.

But while to some extent it was weakened in intensity, it gained very considerably in breadth and liberality, by this universalisation. It helped to prevent the unfortunate divorce between the life of the nation and the larger life of humanity in and through which alone can all national lives and cultures find their highest and most perfect fulfilment and realisation,—the kind of divorce that has happened in Europe.

The rewakening of national consciousness and aspirations in India in our own time has revived the ancient idealism of the Sakti Cult; and Durga,

Kalee, Jagaddhatree, Bhavanee and all the other great forms and symbols used by the Hindu Shakti-worshippers, have received a new meaning. All these old and traditional gods and goddesses who had lost their hold upon the modern mind, have been re-installed with a new historic and nationalist interpretation in the mind and soul of the people. Hundreds of thousands of our people have commenced to hail their mother-land to-day as Durga, Kalee, Jagaddhatree. These are no longer mere mythological conceptions or legendary persons or even poetic symbols. They are different manifestations of the Mother. This Mother is the Spirit of India. This geographical habitat of ours is only the outer body of the Mother. The earth that we tread on is not a mere bit of geological structure. It is the physical embodiment of the Mother. Behind this physical and geographical body there is a Being, a Personality,—the Personality of the Mother. These mountains, these rivers, these extensive plains and lofty plateaus, are all witnesses unto the life and love of our race, in and through which the very life and love of the Mother have sought and found uninterrupted and progressive expression. Our history is the sacred biography of the Mother. Our philosophies are the revelations of the Mother's Mind our arts —our poetry and our painting, our music and our drama, our architecture and our sculpture,all these— are the outflow of the Mother's diverse Emotional Moods and Experiences. Our religion is the organised expression of the Soul of the Mother. The outsider knows her as India. The outsider sees only her outer and lifeless physical frame. The outsider sees her as a mere bit of earth, and looks upon her as only a geographical expression and entity. But we, her children, know her even to-day as our fathers and their fathers had done before, for countless generations, as a Being, as a Manifestation of Prakriti, as our Mother and the Mother of our Race. And we have always, and do still worshiped her as such.

It is, I know, exceedingly difficult, if it be not absolutely impossible, for the European or American to clearly understand or fully appreciate this strange idealisation of our land, which has given birth to this Cult of the Mother among us. Some view it as rank superstition, and some view it as sinister fanaticism. No one has as yet seized, I am afraid, its supreme spiritual significance. And you need not be at all surprised at this. For this Cult of the Mother is based upon the peculiar-ty Hindu conception of what is called the Motherhood of God.

Christianity has preached the Fatherhood of God. The highest Christian piety finds expression in realising God as Father. In all the extensive literature of Christianity there is no attempt to realise God as Mother. The Hindu has always done so. The Hindu Cult of the Mother is no doubt very largely associated with the conception of Prakriti. But in his inner spiritual consciousness the Hindu has realised the Motherhood of God not as a philosophic speculation but as a reality. All our concepts of the Universal are primarily derived from the particularities of personal experience. The Fatherhood of God is, thus, derived from our experiences of human fatherhood,—first in our own fathers, and second, directly, in our own fatherhood when God blesses us with children. Those who have not really known and loved their own father, or have not become fathers themselves, cannot truly know and realise what the Fatherhood of God is. Similarly, it is in the concrete experiences of motherhood in our own mothers first, dimly, as through a glass, and next in the motherhood of our own wives in which we ourselves also so largely participate,—directly and almost face to face, that we can see and seize the Motherhood of God. Besides these two human, personal and primary manifestations of the Divine Motherhood, there are other manifestations also, in Nature, and in Society. Is not the land we live in as much a symbol of the Divine Motherhood even as our own mothers or the mothers of our children are? We are born unto this land. It receives us into its bosom even as our human mothers do. It supports our life with its own substance even as the nursing mother supports the growing life of her own baby. This land is literally the mother of our physical existence. It is indeed the physical body of the soul of our land and nation. Even so is the Society to which we belong, of which this land is the geographical habitat, the vehicle and instrument of the intellectual and spiritual life ot the

Mother-God. From this Society we receive all our mental and spiritual nourishment almost from day to day. And thus, in every way, we are nourished by, dependent upon, draw the strength and inspiration of our physical and mental life from, this complex Being, at once physical and spiritual, geographical and social, which we call and tenderly worship as Mother in our motherland. This Being is as much a revelation of the Motherhood of God as are our human mothers. This is the spiritual basis of the Cult of the Mother among us. It is therefore that our love of our land and people is an organic part of our ideal of the love of God. It is not, like the secular patriotism of Europe, at all a mere civic sentiment.

The Cult of the Mother among us is by no means a political cult. The political propaganda with which the cry of Bande Mataram or Hail Mother, has recently been associated, is not in any sense an organic element of the real Cult of the Mother or Motherland. It is a purely accidental association. And this Cult of the Mother is in no way connected with the impious excesses for which this political propaganda, though, in a very limited and sectional aspect, may be held partly responsible. The type of patriotism that stands really at the back of these excesses is not Hindu or Indian, but essentially an imitation of foreign ideas and ideals, the fruit of the uncritical and undiscriminating study of foreign histories. The real Cult of the Mother among us is part of our general spiritual culture. It is the idealisation and spiritualisation of the collective life and functions of our society. It is the apotheosis of our Race-Spirit and National Organism. It is organically related to our highest conceptions of Humanity.

This Humanity is represented in our thought as Narayana or Mahavishnu. Narayana is an emanation of the Supreme. He is a Being, only differentiated from the Absolute. He is an element of the very Being of God. Both individual humans as well as the collective entity called Humanity, are equally manifestations of Narayana. They are both equally Divine. The one is inseparable from the other, and both from God. And the original form of the Mother, as I have told you, is on the lap of Mahavishnu,—the Nation resting eternally in Humanity. The true Cult of the Mother is, therefore, with us as much a Cult of Nationality as of Humanity. And it is because of this essenial universalism that this Cult of the Mother is so vital a part of our highest religious symbolism and spiritual culture.

LETTER IV.

RELIGIOUS INDIA.

It is only natural that you should be surprised to find such strange affinities between Hinduism and Christianity, as was indicated in my last letter. But, my child, in judging thoughts and systems that are apparently different from that with which we may have been associated, we usually forget that despite these outer differences and conflicts, the Mind that works through these is One. All our thoughts and speculations are the efforts of that One Mind, under different circumstances and in different environment: and, consequently, provided the problems are the same, the solution that the Mind may arrive at in regard to these problems, must also be, though not in form but in any case in essence, the same. Besides the Christian Dogma of the Trinity is admittedly the discovery of the Greek mind, which, as I pointed out to you while discussing the Indian and the European temperament, as you may remember, is structurally the same as the Hindu mind. But even where there are structural differences between the thought of one people and another, even there you will find a high level of spiritual life and thought in both the communities, where their sages and their seers speak the same truths though in diverse languages and through different sets of symbolism. It is only the camp-followers of different Prophets and Teachers, who, failing to understand and visualise the profound meaning of the teachings of their masters, and therefore mistaking the words for the thoughts and the outer forms for the inner spirit, or, in their pride of intellect identifying personal opinions with universal truth and inference with fact, create all the sectarian and denominational conflicts that mark the history of human religion almost everywhere.

BUDDHISM, AND HINDUISM.

Nowhere, I think, have these conflicts been so few and so little ferocious as in India. And perhaps the one root reason of this rare phenomena is to be found in the fact that the dominant religion of India, Hinduism, is not a credal religion like Christianity or Islam. Buddhism that arose out of the early Vedic religion, as a movement of protest against the excessive and soul-killing ritualism of the time, is no doubt a credal religion. But yet it differs, very fundamentally, from the two other credal systems that the world has known. There are two things which distinguish Buddhism from both Christianity and Islam. The first is its strong psychological emphasis, and the second is the absence of that absolutism which is characteristic of both Christianity and Islam. If there be any religion which may claim to be predominantly a Discipline and not a Doctrine, it is, I think, Buddhism. There is, perhaps, no other world-religion which is so little concerned with metaphysical speculations as the religion of Buddha. It asks you to accept nothing that may not be established by pure psychological analysis, and that, consequently, may not be verified by ordinary human experience. And if its assertions are few and simple, its deinals are fewer and very rarely positive. Buddhism has sometimes been characterised as agnostic. That there is a very strong note of agnosticism in the teachings of Buddha can scarcely be denied. But it is an essentially healthy and reasonable kind of agnosticism, The type of agnosticism with which you and I are so familiar in this age, is as dogmatic in its denials of what it does not know as the orthodox Christian or Mahomedan or Hindu is in his assertions of what he professes to believe. The agnosticism of the Buddhist is not of this type. Its verdicts on the claims of other faiths is not that they are false, but simply that they are not-proven. And a credal religion that is characterised by this healthy mental attitude, and is peculiarly free from metaphysical speculations and unverifiable dogmas,—unverifiable, that is, by the ordinary processes of intellection,—must have, inspite of its creed, a very large element of true universalism in it. And all these peculiarities of the Buddhistic credalism that distinguish it from both Christian and Moslem credalism, is entirely due to its nativity. Buddhism is a child of Hinduism, and, therefore, has the dominant characteristics of its parent, namely, its spirit of toleration and universalism.

HINDUISM—NOT A CREED BUT A CULTURE.

Like Bhuddhism, Hinduism is also predominantly a Discipline and a Culture, and not at all a creed. The emphasis of Hinduism is not on what is known as Faith in both Christianity and Islam, but what is called the Path or Pantha in Buddhism. The difference between Buddhism and Hinduism lies in the fact that while in Buddhism there is, practically, an absence of metaphysical speculations, Hinduism does not eliminate these speculations, but tries, rather on the contrary, to seize and realise them as verified and verifiable facts and factors of the deepest spiritual life and experience. Buddhism is essentially agnostic. Hinduism is predominantly gnostic. But it is a gnosticism which does not repudiate and deny but fully accepts and transcends the fundamental facts of agnosticism. In fact the note of Buddhistic agnosticism is derived from the rudimentary agnosticism of the earliest speculations of the Upanishads. In the Upanishads we have :—

It (*i.e.*, the Ultimate Reality) is different from all that we know, and different also from all that we do not know. This is what we have heard from those teachers who explained that (Reality) to us.

And again :—

> Here (*i.e.*, in the attempt to know the Absolute), the injunction is that It is not this, It is not this.
>
> I do not say that I know it. I do not say that I do not know it. He who knows this truly knows.

These are all agnostic utterances. In these the Upanishads practically take up the same position which Buddhism subsequently took up. But while Buddhism stops with this fundamental agnosticism, Hinduism goes further. It says that the Absolute cannot be known in the way in which we know all that is known by us, that is, as *objects* of our knowledge, for to know the Absolute as such and through this method would be to dstroy the very essence of the Absolute as the unrelated and the unconditioned. The things that we know are always conditioned by us as their knower. We are here the subject, and what we know are our object; and the subject always conditions its object. The Absolute cannot be so conditioned. Consequently the Absolute cannot be known *as object*. But in knowing our object we also know ourselves as the subject. As subject we are not conditioned by our object but only condition it. The Absolute may be known, therefore, not as object but as subject. In the Self, through the Self, as the Self,—and even here our language, owing to its native limitations, is really symbolic : for the prepositions, in, through, or as, implying duality and relation, do not apply to the Absolute and the Unrelated,—alone can the Absolute be realised. The final truth, therefore, is :—

> "Shvetaketu That (The Absolute or Brahman) art Thou."

HINDU PANTHEISM.

Europe has labelled all this as Pantheism. And with the easy self-deception of all very clever people, Europe is satisfied in herself that by naming the thing it has fully explained all its mysteries. The popular idea of Pantheism is that everything is God. It is, therefore, regarded as the inevitable parent of Polytheism. And the conclusion is, on the face of it, absolutely irresistible. For, if everything be God, then there are as many Gods as there are things. Pantheism and Polytheism are therefore only two sides of the same thing. But this popular interpretation of Pantheism is European, and not Indian. It is only when you accept the reality of what you call "everything,"—that is, the truth of the separate entities of these different things,—it is only upon this hypothesis, that you can establish Polytheism upon Pantheism. But the Hindu never accepted the reality of the phenomenal world. What the philosophers call the manifold of experience, has always been dismissed as unreal by Hindu speculations. To the Hindu both the 'every-ness" and the "thingness," that is, both the isolation and the reality of what the European calls everything, are only apparent and not real, have truth and being only on the lower Practical or Vyavaharic plane, as Samkara would say, but not on the plane of Reality, or the Paramarthic plane, as he calls it. So you will see, that even the School of Absolute Monism in India does not understand by Pantheism what Christendom generally understands by that term.

WHAT IS THE "THOU"?

And the real reason of it is that the European has only known the word, but has rarely or never tried to seize the fundamental concept which the word conveys. The Hindu had fully seized that concept. And you too may seize it if you clearly analyse your own thought-life. When, in answer to the query :—"What is Brahman or the Absolute ?"—the Guru replied, "Shvetaketu, That art thou," what is it that he referred to as "thou" in that answer ? It was not the body of Svetaketu. The Hindu consciousness had, almost from prehistoric times, realised the distinction between the soul and the body. Neither could the Teacher refer by "thou" to the intellect of Shvetaketu, for in Hindu Psychology, the intellect is itself one of the senses, the eleventh sense. It is called manas in Sanskrit. The function of the manas is to seize the meaning of the senses, to distinguish one sensation from another, and to thus make knowledge of sensuous objects possible. The manas or the intellect lives and works in duality and difference. Nether is this "thou" the emotions or the will of Svetaketu, for both our emotions and our will, like our intellect, live upon the sense of division and duality, and cannot therefore be the Absolute. And when our physical, our intellectual, our emotional, and our volitional life,—all these are eliminated as not identical with the Absolute, then what else is it that remain in us? Is there anything that is still left or not? And if there is, such a thing, what is it ? That is the real question. If we can discover that something, we may then know what it is that the Guru spoke of as "thou" when saying,—"Svetaketu That (or the Absolute or Brahman) art thou."

"THE WITNESS" IN US.

Now our senses, our intellect, our emotions and our will, all these are working perpetual changes in us. But we are all the same always conscious of the fact that inspite of all these changes we are really one and the same. Indeed, unless we were the same in and through these constant changes, we could never have known even these very changes themselves. There must be something in us which bears witness unto all these changes. And the witness of a series of changes must be such as, though present in the changes, is not itself affected, that is changed, by them. Not one single experience of ours, whether sensuous or intellectual or emotional or volitional, is at all explicable except upon the hypothesis that there is this witness in us, which is changeless in the midst of changes, unrelated in the midst of relations, unconditioned in the midst of infinite conditions,—which is Eternal and Absolute. It is this thing in us, which constitutes our true Self, to which the Guru referred Svetaketu when he said—"That art thou." In fact if we only could detatch ourselves from ourselves, free our consciousness from the false identification of our self with the changing sensations of our body, or the alternating consciousness and semiconsciousness and unconsciousness which is the condition of our intellectual life, or with the fitful flow of our emotions or the impulsions and repulsions of our will,—if we could detach our self from these, then we would at once see that in every act of knowledge, as well as in every movement of our affections and our will, we are constantly creating and cancelling the dualities through which these work, and are reaching out to that in us which is, really, the Absolute. Through this absolute self-detachment it is possible to reach the state in which all duality is cancelled, all differentiations cease, where there is neither object nor subject, neither knower nor known,—and therefore, no knowledge either, as we understand knowledge on the lower intellectual plane,—but there is still Consciousness. We are perpetually reaching this Consciousness, but are driven out of it immediately we get into it, by the outward movement of our senses and our intellect, our emotions and our will. But those who are called Yogis in our literature, so discipline their senses, their mind, their emotions and their will, that these outward movements, natural to the senses, the intellect, the emotions and the will, are brought absolutely under control, and so these Yogis can remain in this state of superconsciousness as long as they desire. It is these people only who know and truly understand what the Guru meant when he said, in reply to the disciple's question,—"What is Brahman ?"—"Svetaketu That art thou."

THE KEY TO THE HINDU RELIGION.

And I am taking you through this dry and abstruse analysis, because it is here that you will find the real key to our religion. From what I have, very perfunctorily, stated above, you will see that even the most abstruse speculations of the Hindus are not mere speculations as speculation is understood in Europe. They are based upon positive, inner experience, and are, therefore, as much verifiable through their specific methods as are the truths of what claim in our day to be positive sciences.

THE SCIENTIFIC CHARACTER OF HINDUISM.

In fact, I am not aware of any other world-religion which may claim to be so scientific, as the religion of the Hindus. It is, I think, the only religion of an advanced type, that seeks absolute verification, in actual experience, of its most abstruse faith and speculations. The Hindu wants nothing to be taken for granted, nay not even the universal theistic faith in a Supreme Being, who is the Author and Governor of the Universe. Hinduism wants every man to rise to his own faith through his own efforts. The Hindu teacher, like the capable modern pedagogue, trained in the most advanced methods of the pedagogy of our time, always tries to gently guide him to the truth; but never to forcibly impose his own ideas and opinions upon his pupil. This has been our orthodox method of spiritual training from very ancient times. And it is, therefore, that we have such endless diversities of faiths and practices in our religion, due to diversities of mental and spiritual endowments and acquisitions. This specific Hindu method of religious training is very lucidly illustrated in the story of Varuna and his son Bhrigu, recorded in the Taittiriya Upanishad.

THE BHRIGU-VARUNA EPISODE.

Bhrigu, the son of the sage Varuna, so runs this story, one day went to his father and said, "Teach me, O revered one, the knowledge of Brahman." Varuna said:—"Seek to know Brahman through meditation." And with a view to help him to meditate properly, he indicated what Brahman is with this text:—

> "That from which all that exist have come into being; that by which after coming to being, all that are, continue to be; that towards which all objects move and into which all objects enter;—know That as Brahman."

You will thus see that the Teacher here does not present to his pupil his own conclusions regarding Brahman or the Ultimate Reality. He does not impose his own faith or idea upon him; but simply gives him a problem in equation, so to say, and wants him to solve it for himself. The Brahman is as yet unknown to the pupil. And the teacher keeps this character even in his own instruction. He speaks of Brahman here in the terms of what is called in Algebra, X and Y,—in the terms of the unknown. Only what he does to help his son and pupil is to place this unknown quantity, this X or Y, in relation to three known quantities, namely, birth, life and death. These are matters of universal experience. Things that were not, come to be, this, in the case of living things, is called birth. Then things that come into being continue to be, this is life. Things that are, pass out of existence, this is what, in the case of humans and animals, we call death. These three things are matters of universal experience. Theist, atheist, agnostic, everybody has these three-fold experience. And Varuna here presents Brahman in relation to this universal experience. These are the known quantities of this equation. The unknown is Brahman. And Bhrigu was asked to find out the value of this unknown quantity, by meditation.

And he started his meditation with the analysis of these three universal experiences. And the first result that he got was that "Annam (literally, Food) was Brahman." Food here really stands for the material basis of the universe. The conclusion that the Ultimate Reality is Food, means really, in terms of the modern mind, that it is matter. It is the final verdict of the physico-chemical group of the sciences. That "Annam is Brahman." is the universal verdict of materialism both ancient and modern. Nay more, it is the highest generalisation of the group of experiences which are examined and analysed by the physical sciences. It is not an absolutely false conclusion, either. Under certain mental conditions, however much we may pretend to do otherwise, we cannot by any means get beyond the material interpretation of experience. To those who are on this plane of intellectual and spiritual evolution, you can easily give, what to you are higher and fuller generalisations, as you may make a Christmas-present of a rich fur-coat to a friend, but can never create any real and living religious conviction. No amount of dogmatic instruction will be able to lift them out of these materialistic conclusions. They themselves must, with their own efforts, through further and deeper analysis of their own experience, and the fuller examination of their conclusions in the light of these new analyses and experiences, get out of these conclusions, however crude they may seem to others. And Varuna followed this rational method. When his son came and told him that he had found Brahman and that it was Food or Annam, he said again, as before :—"By meditation seek to know Brahman."

The first conclusion that Varuna reached was that "Food is Brahman." By food he evidently meant the material basis of life. The phenomena of birth with which he was familiar referred to the human, or at most to the animal kingdom. What we call Nature is apparently unborn and deathless. So Bhrigu started his analysis of experience with the familiar human kingdom. And here he saw that the fœtus grows through the food taken by the mother, during gestation. After birth, it is food again that maintains life. At death the body becomes the food of others. So he arrived at the conclusion that Food is Brahman. The form of it may be primitive and crude, but Bhrigu's first conclusion here regarding the Ultimate Reality is really the universal conclusion, as I have already said, of all materialistic hypothesis of the universe. It is the conclusion of the physical sciences. Food here stands for matter. Having reached this conclusion, Bhrigu went to his father and said that he had found Brahman: Food is Brahman. The father said:—"By meditation seek to know Brahman."

Bhrigu went and commenced to meditate again. And now he started with an analysis of the first conclusion, that Food is Brahman. Now, food is only for the living, and not for the dead. So it is life and not food, from which beings are born, by which beings are made to live, and finally it is another life that beings go to and enter. So he went and told his father:—"Life is Brahman." Even as we in our own time, rise from the physical to the biological plane, in our progressive analysis of experience, so did Bhrigu. And his conclusion was, indeed, the universal conclusion of the Biological group of the sciences. His father rejected this also, and said:—"By meditation seek to know Brahman."

So Bhrigu once again commenced to meditate, and rose in the next step from Biology to Psychology, from life or prana to Manas or the sensorium, as the ultimate principle in creation. Manas is Brahman, he went and told his father. The father said :—" Seek to know Brahman by meditation." Bhrigu went to meditate again, and as the result of the analysis of the psychological explanation of experience, he found that what is called the Unity of Consciousness, which is the subject especially of philosophic speculation, this is a higher principle. Psychology cannot explain itself without Philosophy, as Biology cannot explain itself without Psychology, nor even Physico-Chemical Sciences without Biology. In this Unity of Consciousness, Bhrigu thought he found the solution of his problem. There was, however, one order of experience that had not been touched by any of the analyses so far made by Bhrigu. The

Unity of Consciousness or Bijnanam as it is called in Sanskrit, explains as far as our intellectual life : but it cannot offer any rational ground or explanation of our emotional life. Least of all can it explain the *raison d'être* of the phenomenal world. This he found, finally, in what he called Anandam, roughly rendered into English by Joy or Love.

"From Anandam have all these things come into heing, having come into being, by Anandam are they kept alive, towards Anandam do they move and into Anandam do they enter."

Anandam is Brahman. This was the final conclusion at which Bhrigu arrived, as the result of these progressive analyses of experience.

I will not carry you through the further analysis to which the concept Anandam was subjected, and upon which the whole Philosophy of the School of Love and Faith in Hinduism is based. My main idea in citing this interesting old story here is to indicate what I have already described as the cultural character of the Hindu religion, as distinguished from the credal character of Christianity or Islam.

HINDUISM—A CULTURE, NOT A CREED.

The endless diversities of faiths and rituals that are found in our religion, are entirely due to this cause. Modern pedagogy works upon the principle that the course and character of the training of every student must be determined by his or her individual endowments and tendencies, and consequently any attempt to bring all students under any one uniform system is fatal to true intellectual life and evolution. A healthy and rational system of education must study and recognise individual peculiarities and suit itself to these. Hinduism has always tried to follow this principle in regard to spiritual training and culture. Dogmas and creeds may to some extent be imposed from the outside: but real piety must grow from within. And what is to be developed from within must work upon the inner nature of the person in whom it is to grow. And as men's inner nature differs in the case of different people, so their religious duties and disciplines must also be different. What may be helpful to one person may not be helpful to another. There cannot be, therefore, any universal creed or any uniform ritual in a religion that seeks not to preach opinion but to grow character.

THE UNIVERSAL REFERENCE OF THE BHRIGU-VARUNA EPISODE.

The story of Bhrigu, however, not only indicates the cultural character of Hinduism, but has, it seems to me, a much wider reference and meaning. Bhrigu here may well stand for the whole of humanity. And the way in which he rose gradually from one conclusion to another in his search after God or the Absolute, may well be taken as presenting the complete history of the evolution of religion. His first conclusion, as I have already told you, is the universal conclusion of Materialism. This Materialism is not a special product of our age. Modern science is not the real parent of it either. Our scientific investigations and discoveries have added certain new forms to the materialistic interpretation of the universe, but the spirit that stands behind it is as old as the human race. Indeed, as we see in the story of Bhrigu, it is the earliest result of the application of the opening intelligence of man to the solution of the problem of the universe. It took, God alone knows how many milleniums, for man to see anything beyond what his senses revealed. And the senses never can of themselves, take us further than what Bhrigu called Annam or Food. Of course the senses themselves loudly repudiate their pretensions to any form of finality. They seem to be perpetually crying, as much in our rational life, through the intellect ; as in our emotional life, through the unquenchable thirst of our heart ; that they are not an end unto themselves. But who hears their ceaseless warnings ? It needs long and tedious disciplines to hear what the senses are always telling us. It took thousands of years for man to catch the first faintest note of this constant warning. And even now he has heard only a mere echo of it. And as long as we are completely under the spell of the senses, so long the only possible realisation of the Absolute by us must be in the form in which Bhrigu realised it. We may not call it, after him, Annam but Electron, not Food but Force. But by whatever name called the reality is the same. In fact, it can hardly be denied that one of the most prominent results of our modern scientific achievements has been to quicken the powers of our senses both by natural and artificial means, and thereby to extend our sensuous hold on the universe. And in proportion as we extend our sense-domination over phenomena, in that proportion our sense-life also extends and strengthens its dominion over us. Our servants, thus, always become our masters. Modern science instead of weakening, has, therefore, visibly strengthened the hold of the material world over our mind. And one of the signs of this renewed domination of matter over mind in our age, is seen in the increasing materialisation of our old spiritual concepts. Both in England and America there has grown up in course of the last quarter of a century a new group of terms that seeks to express the profoundest experiences of our inner life in the technique of the physical sciences. And in view of this increasing materialisation of our thoughts, how can we possibly reach out to the profound mysteries of the spiritual life unless it be through mere material concepts? The Hindu has always recognised the impossibility of transcending the limitations of our nature except through following the inner bents and trends of that nature itself. Those who are completely under the domination of the sensuous can rise gradually to the consciousness of the spiritual only through these very senses themselves. The senses must, by some means or other, be supernaturalised for them. It is through this supernaturalisation of the senses that these people can gradually rise to the faith in the supersensuous. This is the secret of the so-called idolatry of the Hindus. It is, of course, only one of the aspects of this complex culture. It has many other aspects, of which I shall speak D. V.—later on. The Hindu's so-called worship of stocks and stones has been admittedly ordained for this purpose, namely, to lead him through the senses to the contemplation of the supersensuous. And what these so-called stocks and stones do for the ordinary Hindu, Occultism and Spiritism are seeking to do for the modern European and American. Occultism and Spiritism, whatever may or may not be the exact measure of truth in these, mean really the manifestation of spiritual phenomena on the physical plane and the interpretation of the supersensuous in the terms of the senses. Those who have truly risen to the vision of the spiritual do not need these signs and wonders to create or confirm their faith in the Unseen. But these signs and wonders are however needed to create and confirm the faith of those who lack real spiritual acquisitions. The same thing is true of the ordinary Hindu worshipper also. He is still completely under the domination of his senses. The first thing to do for him, to create a sense of the supersensuous, is to gradually train his mind to habits of detatchment from the sensuous. And these habits are cultivated by two means. One of these is to establish the domination of the will over the impulses and activities of the senses ; and the other is to train the mind to see the Unseen in the seen.

PHYSICAL PURITY : CLEANLINESS.

The first of these is called in the literature of Hinduism, deha-shuddhi. Deha means the body, and shuddhi purification. The purification of the body is the first step in Hindu culture. The Hindu had realised, ages and ages before the modern man, the close and organic interdependence between our body and our mind. Physiological Psychology, almost a new discovery in modern Europe, has been a very old science in this country. And it is because the Hindu had fully realised the organic dependence of our mind and morals upon the state of our body, and more particularly upon that of our nerves, that he has always insisted upon a course of psycho-physical disciplines and practices as an absolute condition-precedent of the growth of morals as well as of the true spiritual life. Deha-shuddhi, or purification of the body is the common name of this course of psycho-physical disciplines. The personal cleanliness, characteristic of the Hindu, is the fruit of these agelong disciplines. The Hindu is, therefore, admittedly, the most clean animal in the human kingdom. This cleanliness means not only that he is a much-washed animal, but that he observes most punctilliously this law of cleanliness in whatever he does. If the Hindu touches his own lips with his hand, the hand becomes impure, and he cannot touch anything, neither food nor raiment, without carefully and completely washing that hand. The clothes that he puts on while going to the outer world, whether it be the court or the market or the house of a friend even, cannot, strictly speaking, be taken back into the living rooms of his house, until they are thoroughly washed and dried. For cleanliness, a Hindu's house has always the sanctified odour of a temple. The Englishman's house, they say, is his castle: the Hindu's house, my child, is his temple. It is holy ground. So, like Moses, he always takes off his boots when he enters its precincts. Like his person, his food also must always be religiously clean. The Hindu's ideal of cleanliness has apparently a lot to do with the restrictions imposed by his religion in the matter of both food and drink. There are Hindus to whom all manner of animal food is prohibited. But even those to whom these restrictions have not been extended, are not allowed to take every kind of meat. The deer is regarded as the purest of animals. Consequently venison is the most approved meat. Pork is absolutely prohibited owing to the character of the swine. But the same objection does not apply to the wild boar, against which therefore there is no such rigid restriction. The Bengali Hindu is not allowed to take domestic fowls, but the wild species is not prohibited. So in regard to fishes also, those of observed unclean habits are avoided. The prohibition of beef as well as of the meat of the females of all animals, is due to other causes. The prohibition of fermented drinks is also partly due to considerations of cleanliness. Many of our domestic habits and social usages had their origin in this religious regard of the Hindu for the quality of cleanliness. The pious Hindu takes his meals not out of porcelain or metallic plates but out of banana-leaves that may be thrown away every time they are used. On festive occasions, when guests are invited by scores and hundreds, the use of the banana-leaves for plates is universal, not merely because of the difficulty of providing so many plates, but for the graver reason that when a person eats out of a metallic plate, it becomes impure, and can only be purified by burning it in a forge. The Hindu seems to have always known it that many an infectious disease passes from one person to another through the excretions of the mouth. The sputum has always been regarded by him almost as impure as the excreta. He never tolerated therefore in his social intercourse the civilised practice of osculation. The crusade against osculation as a prolific medium of many diseases just started in Europe and America, was therefore never needed in India.

These disciplines of cleanliness have however not merely a physical or hygeinic value but have always been regarded by the Hindu as necessary to his religious and spiritual life also. Modern civilisation has long treated these disciplines as survivals of old-world superstitions. It is however, to be hoped that the progress of psycho-physical and psychological researches and the consequent recognition of the organic interdependence of our mind and our body will gradually lead even the civilised man to understand and appreciate the ethical reference of the physical disciplines of Hinduism.

"INSTRUCTIVE" AND "CONSTRUCTIVE."

This ethical reference of the apparently external and physical disciplines of Hinduism has scarcely been recognised by the European or American student of our life and institutions. Even our own modern-educated classes have frequently found it difficult to do so. The inevitable formalism of the essentially forensic character of Christian ethics is largely responsible for this misunderstanding. An excessive emphasis on the dogma of the freedom of the human will on the one hand, and a more or less complete ignorance of the organic interdependence between our nerves and the inhibitive powers of our will on the other, have combined to create this formalism, and to make Christian ethics predominantly instructive. Like the Christian religion, Christian morals also are propagated through the usual missionary method of preaching or instruction. You have therefore ethical text-books and elaborately-equipped Sunday Schools, for imparting moral instructions to the young all over Europe and America. The Christian pulpit tries to do the same work for the adults and the elders of the community. What the Sunday School teacher or the Christian Minister does is simply to proclaim what is right and should be done, and then practically to leave the duty of doing the right to the individuals concerned. If they are able to do so, they receive their due meed of approbation and praise ; if they fail they receive the condemnation and punishment which is their due. Everything, you will thus see, is practically left in the matter of the right regulation of conduct, to the chances of individual effort and strength. Christian ethics has so far taken little notice of the constitutional capacities or incapacities of human individuals in regard to the ethical life. Differences of physical or intellectual endowments are recognised, and, where necessary, generously condoned. But Christendom has not as yet given almost any recognition to original moral endowments. It is only very recently that Lombroso and the School of Criminal Anthropology of which he was the father, have discovered the congenital character of the criminal propensities of at least a certain class of instinctive criminals. These propensities are constitutional and organic and cannot be cured without a change in the organism itself. Hindu Psychology had recognised from of old, this organic character of man's moral aptitudes and virtuous impulses.

It has always recognised the fact that both our real intellectual and our true moral life are largely established upon our nervous system. Difference of personal temperaments,—one is phlegmatic and another impassioned, one is hard to irritate and another is quick to resent, one is excessively sensitive to sex-impulse and another almost impervious to it, one is selfish another generous, one is cringy another free-handed,—all these are constitutional, and are related to very subtle differences in different nerve-structures. Fully recognising these facts of common experience, the Hindu has always been naturally slow to condemn and punish and ready to condone and forgive the wrong-doer. The forensic formalism of Christian ethics has developed a somewhat keener sense of personal responsibility in the European than what is usually seen in the Indian. The psychological realism of Hindu ethics has to a large extent prevented the growth of any strong sense of moral responsibility in the Indian. On the other hand, his keen sense of personal responsibility has made the European so impatient of people's weaknesses and intolerant of their misdeeds ; while the general weakness of this sense in the Hindu has made him divinely patient of people's faults and foibles, and uniformly tolerant of all human wrongs. The soul of ethics in the Hindu character is therefore not what is called the conscience in Christian literature, but rather love. And the real basis of it is our nerve-organisation.

THE ETHICS OF PSYCHO-PHYSICS.

Hindu ethics has always fully recognised this fact. Psycho-physical disciplines have, therefore, formed so fundamental a part of the moral and religious training of the Hindu. The purification of deha or the physical body, called also bhuta-suddhi in

Sanskrit, of which I have just spoken, formed, therefore, the very first step in this training. The daily baths and ablutions, as well as the various restrictions regarding food and drinks, have an admitted psycho-physical reference. All food is divided in our books into three classes : the highest of these is that which is recommended to the Brahmins, those whose special function is to lead and shape the soul-life of the people. They must themselves be supremely spiritual. And the proper food for the spiritually minded people is, that which is sweet, and fatty (has vegetable fat in it), and substantial and pleasant to take. This is the class of food that contributes to health and strength, happiness and long life and vigour and virility. The next class of food consists of things that are bitter, acid, have too much salt, is too warm or dry or pungent or hot. This is the class of food that is proper for the warrior class ; it causes pain and bereavement. That which has stood overnight, the flavour natural to which is lost, which is decomposed, or consists of the leavings of other people's plates, or which is forbidden to be used in sacrifices ; these are the last class of food. This class of food contributes to inertia and animalism, and is liked only by those whose nature is essentially very low and vicious. The Hindu realised that what we eat or drink has a very great influence upon the condition of our inner life. Certain kinds of food inevitably quicken our animalities. That drinks of a certain class do this is universally recognised even by the modern man : why cannot then our foods have also the same effect ? Meat, for instance, produces certain inner tendencies that are not produced by pure vegetables. I remember one of your publicists proclaiming some years ago that the superiority of the European, as a fighting animal over the non-European, was largely, if not entirely, due to the beef-and-beer consuming capacity of the former. Though for many many centuries past the Hindu has prohibited beef, it will be interesting to you to be told that both meat and strong drinks have always been freely permitted by the Hindu Scriptures to those whose special function in the social organism has been to fight and rule. Our restrictions regarding food and drink have thus a far more than a mere physical or hygeinic reference.

In fact, to fully understand, even where it may not be possible for the modern consciousness to fully support, the complicated restrictions enjoined upon the Hindu in regard to what is called interdining, we must view these in the light of Hindu Psychophysics. The conclusions of this science as the Hindu understood and investigated it, may have to be largely modified by the larger experiences and investigations of our day, but we cannot entirely ignore the fundamental basis of these restrictions. The Hindu refuses to eat food cooked by certain classes. The original reason of this prohibition was absolutely psych-ophysical. These classes were at one time really unclean in their habits and very low in their manner of living. They made no discrimination between food and drinks,—between those that were likely to be conducive, and those that were likely to be prejudicial, to the higher life. In fact, even in our own day most of these classes or castes, are more or less careless in regard to personal cleanliness. They scarcely observe the almost universal Hindu rule concerning the contamination of food and drink through contact with what is called in Sanskrit, uchchhistam, or what has been left after eating or drinking by others. These are people who eat out of each other's plates or drink out of each other's glass, or who, in other ways, are not very particular about the contact, either direct or remote, of food stuffs with the sputum of people. These are people who eat all kinds of forbidden foods and indulge in all kinds of prohibited drinks. But the Hindu believes, whether rightly or wrongly, that it is not merely the sputum of people that contaminates foods and drinks, but even their very breath, which carries with it microscopic particles of their inner organs, is also a source of such contamination; especially when it comes through the mouth. It is, therefore, that you will see, in truly orthodox households, the cook, even though a man or woman of the highest caste, ties a piece of clean cloth over the lips to prevent the breath coming even into the suspicion of any contact with the dishes cooked by him or her. These restrictions, though carried like many things else, by our people to what may seem irrational excesses, have, however, this psycho-physical reference.

These do not, however, mean in any sense whatever, any hatred of the classes with regard to whom they have to be observed. In fact, these restrictions apply under certain circumstances even to the members of one's own family. In every orthodox Hindu family, not even the mistress or the daughter of the house is permitted to enter the kitchen or touch any food or drink without having previously bathed and changed her usual clothings. And it is because these rules regarding personal purity were not strictly observed by every class or caste, that taking food from those who did not observe them, was prohibited to those who did.

Indeed, it seems clear from our ancient records that at one time these restrictions did not at all apply as between one higher caste and another. The Brahmins used at one time to freely partake of food cooked by the Kshetriyas, for instance; and the prohibition did not apply, I think, even to the Vaisyas. All these three were called the twice-born castes. The laws of personal cleanliness were the same among all these three castes. And, consequently, there was no objection to their dining with one another. These restrictions came in much later, when, I think, the neighbouring non-Aryan communities commenced to be taken into the Aryan fold, and with this expansion there entered a large variety of different stocks with different habits and customs, into the common Aryan Society. Be that, however, as it may, all these outer and physical or physiological restrictions and disciplines have, in the eye of the Hindu, a distinct ethical value. The Hindu believes in the organic character of the ethical life. It is by no means so absolutely self-determined as it is generally regarded by many people. The Bhagavadgeeta says, as you may perhaps remember, that the actual agent of what we claim as our acts is not one, but five, and these five agents are responsible for everything we do. These are:—(i) our body, (ii) our self or the empirical ego as the philosophers would say, (iii) our senses, (iv) the multifarious efforts that we make to realise our purpose, and (v) the impulse of the Divine. All our acts are the joint product of these. And this being so, it is sinful perversity, says the Geeta, to look upon the self as the only agent.

MORAL EDUCATION.

True moral education, therefore, the Hindu says, must involve the training and regulation of all these five agencies that combine and co-operate with one another, to originate all our activities and work up our conduct in life. The relation between these five agencies is rather one of co-ordination than that of the subordination of some to the domination of others. In the higher stages of evolution, the more spiritual of these agencies do control the less spiritual, it is true; and at last, the self, freed by long course of disciplines from the bondage of the senses and all their outer stimuli, can and do exercise almost complete sovereignty over them. But this stage is reached when the education of the self is completed, and not when it is only started or is progressing. As long as this high stage is not reached, our body and our senses, our intellect, our emotions, and our will, and the outer stimuli that are constantly quickening these, all act and react upon one another, and it is impossible or next to impossible to control and regulate any one of these five-fold agencies that are jointly responsible for our moral life, without simultaneously controlling and regulating the others. And it should be recognised that these various agencies have a certain measure of what may be called local autonomy, each within its own proper sphere. The body and the senses, for instance, have this autonomy within the limits of the physical and the sense-life. No one can, therefore, neglect the laws of physiology or psycho-physics, and yet expect, by sheer exercise of the will, to control their inner propensities or their outer actions. Is it not absolute folly, my child, to demand a sort of anarchist freedom in the matter of what one shall eat or drink, or what life one shall lead, in regard to one's physical or sense-activities, and at the same time hope to attain the highest ethical ends? Those who cherish these fancies, either do not know or they do not bear it in mind, that our foods and drinks, our associations and conversations, our works and our recreations, all these are constantly helping or hindering the growth of healthy nerve-tissues, which form really the very plinth and foundation of our moral life. And it is in the light of these that we must study and understand the complex outer ordinances and regulations of the religious life of the Hindu. There may possibly be many errors of observation in the system of Hindu psycho-physics, upon which these externalities of the Hindu's religion are based. The more thorough and scientific investigations of our age may discover these errors and remove them. But these are matters of detail, which do not in the least destroy the fundamental Hindu position that true moral education must be essentially constructive and not merely instructive as it is predominantly in Christendom. And the more you know and understand the Hindu system of ethics, the more, I think, my child, you will see the need of largely amending the fundamentally forensic formalism of what proudly proclaims itself as high and superior Christian ethics. In fact the close psycho-physical reference of ethical culture is not entirely unknown even to Christian or

Moslem experiences either. Indeed the psycho-physical disciplines of Hinduism, are not exclusively Hindu. Almost all the old-world religions had them. We find these in Judaism. They were fully recognised as essential to the higher religious and spiritual culture, by the Catholic Church. They are found in Islam. The main difference in regard to this matter between Hinduism on the one side, and Christianity or Islam on the other, lies in this, namely, that while in the former these are enjoined upon all or almost all classes : in the latter systems they are almost entirely confined to the higher cultures of the saints and devotees. In other words, that which has been organised into social and socio-religious institutions among us, exists only as special disciplines for the monks aud dervishes in the Christian or the Moslem world.

THE EDUCATION OF THE WILL.

There is, however, another aspect of these socio-religious disciplines of

Hinduism, which also should be carefully considered. The injunctions and prohibitions of Hinduism in regard to the utmost outer concerns of man's life, have a very salutary effect upon his character by helping to strengthen the inhibitive powers of the will, as well as by training the individual to perpetually give preference in his daily work and recreations to the good over the pleasant. The range of what is usually called personal freedom in Christendom, but which practically means so often the range of the unrestrained use and indulgence of the senses, is almost infinitely more limited in the socio-religious life of the Hindu than in that of the Christian, especially of the advanced Protestant, and more especially of the conscientious Nonconformist. Even what are regarded as absolutely legitimate enjoyment of the senses by our Christian or Mahomedan friends, are hedged in, by the socio-religious law of the Hindus, by numerous restrictions.

Not only there are certain kinds of food absolutely prohibited, but even where a particular class of edibles are not so tabooed, there even, the use of these is forbidden on particular days of the lunar month. Certain vegetables, for instance, are forbidden in certain tithis or phases of the moon. On the face of it, this class of restrictions seems to be utterly irrational. But if you look at these from the view-point of real ethical training, namely, as exercises in self-control, I think, even we, who are so steeped in the spirit of what so proudly proclaims itself as modern rational life, shall have to concede some ethical value to them. The Bengalee Hindu who is allowed to take meat, cannot kill an animal, strictly speaking, for his own delectation. It is the meat of animals that have been duly sacrificed which alone is permissible, and not butcher's meat. And is it possible even for the most conceited rationalist to deny the salutariness of this restriction ?

It works in a twofold way, the animal that is to be sacrificed, must in the first place be absolutely clean and healthy. You cannot sacrifice lean and worn-out or diseased and dying animals ; and then partake of its meat. In the next place, there are special places, or particular occasions, and appointed hours which you cannot create, when alone can these sacrifices be held. And all these help to curb and control your desire for animal food even when your religion may not altogether prohibit it. As in the matter of our palates, so also in regard to the other senses. The Hindu has always recognised that the desire for food and for procreation are the two strongest sense-impulses in humanity. And, consequently, he has hedged in even the perfectly legitimate satisfaction of both these impulses by the most minute restrictions. St. Paul fully realised the importance of these restraints in regard to the sex-relation, when he said that even the married shall live as if they were unmarried. The Hindu did not leave so vital a matter affecting as much the life of the individual as of the society of which he may be a member, to be guided merely by the moral sense or the inhibitive power of the will of the individual, working within the general limitations of the marital relation. He has ordained numerous laws and restrictions to secure the healthy exercise of this vital function, calculated to simultaneously secure the health of both the individual and the race. The Hindu who has not been liberalised from the bondage of his national religion and superstitions, still lives for more than half the days of each month, in obedience to these injunctions, even when he is married, as if he were unmarried. It is for this reason, that the modern civilised problem of what the American Press was so keenly discussing some years ago, as the problem prostitution in married life, is as yet an unknown problem among us, except possibly, in a very insignificant section of those who have commenced to be civilised after the European model. It is, of course, a rather new problem even in the West, which owes its origin to the general decadence of Christian faith and the decline of the old influence of healthy Christian disciplines over the life of the modern man, in Christendom.

You will thus see, that in the socio-religious life of the Hindu there is a much narrower range for the indulgence of the senses and the appetites than there is, perhaps, in any other system. The Hindu has to submit to much greater restraints even in what is regarded as quite legitimate enjoyments everywhere, than the votaries of the other great world-religions. Not only are there numerous fast days in every month, but on the day previous to every domestic celebration, the master of the family has to fast partially and abstain from even the permissible enjoyments of life. The Hindu celebrates the anniversary of the death of his parents and of his grand parents also, as a sacred religious ceremony. And he has to observe both the day of the ceremony as well as that preceding it, as a sacred day, when he must abstain from all manner of sense-enjoyments whether in regard to food and drink or other matters, and devote the whole time to the contemplation of the higher life. On these days he must not take his ordinary meals or his usual food; must not be engaged in games of any kind; must not speak harsh words to any one, or indulge even in legitimate conjugal association, or in any other way give the least latitude to his senses and appetites. There are numerous days in the year dedicated to different gods and goddesses, and those who worship them, have to observe similar disciplines on these occasions. It is by these means that the general socio-religious scheme of the Hindus, help materially to advance the real ethical life of the people. It is to these that we owe all the humanity of our national character. Our proverbial patience and mildness; our admitted respect for all life, both human and non-human; our special spiritual aptitudes, and our general freedom from some of the most obtrusive vices of civilised humanity; all these are largely due to these socio-religious institutions and the physico-ethical disciplines associated with them, which are so often dismissed by the modern man both in Europe and even in India, as mere superstitions.

MASTERY OVER NATURE.

And the fundamental object of all these restraints and regulations is to train the mind to habits of self-control and self-detachment, and, thereby, to free it from the universal bondage of Nature. Strictly speaking, the attainment of an absolute mastery over Nature is the central idea of all these disciplines. The European also is anxious for the attainment of this mastery. All the superior claims of the modern European civilisation over the older civilisations of the world, are based upon the wonderful mastery that Europe thinks she has been able to establish over Nature through her advanced scientific attainments. That, of course, is a kind of mastery, no doubt. But, frankly speaking, my child, it has often seemed to me like the mastery of the valet over his own lord and master. The valet studies the weak points of his master, and exercises immense control over him through these weaknesses. Is not Europe's control over Nature, very largely of this character ? Europe has been investigating the laws of Nature, has been discovering the secrets through which Nature works in her own dominions ; and by operating upon Nature through these secrets, Europe is compelling Nature to serve the increasingly expansive material ends of her children. But the process, however clever and comendable, does not at all touch even the outermost fringe of the fundamental problem that man's intimate relations with outer Nature creates. Indeed, Europe seems to have almost completely lost the very consciousness of that fundamental problem. And because Europe has practically lost sight of it, she is heaping problems upon problems, and complications upon complications, in her march of progress, without being able to even remotely suggest any remedy or solution for these. Scientific conquest of Nature has immensely increased the material wealth of Europe. And this increased material prosperity has enormously increased the material wants of her children also : but has it advanced their manhood, or even their happiness ? In seeking to establish a larger and larger mastery over Nature through the advancement of the Natural Sciences, has not Europe been increasingly losing her own self-mastery? Indeed, this proud conquest of outer Nature has, it seems to me, its compensation in a corresponding conquest of the soul of man by his senses.

The Hindu had analysed his relations with outer Nature more thoroughly than what the European has perhaps as yet done. The Hindu saw that Nature's hold upon him was only through his senses and his appetites. Here, in his sense-life, lay the root of the cruel domination of Nature over man. The way of science, such as is being so diligently followed in Europe, is really not to curtail but continually to extend and strengthen the dominion of outer Nature over man's sense-life. The practical application of the laws of science for removing human wants, means increased satisfaction of the senses. And this increased service of the senses increases inevitably the hold over man, of what is called "the world, the flesh, and devil," in your popular parlance. And these increased demands of the senses upon the attention and activities of man, mean not the diminution but rather a corresponding increase of Nature's true mastery over us. The Hindu knew all this ; and, therefore, he did not follow this suicidal plan in the evolution of his culture and civilisation. In the face of his ancient records it is not possible to argue that he never tried to study and discover the secrets of Nature. Dr. Prafulla Chandra Ray's recent publication, the History of Hindu Chemistry, and especially Principal Brajendra Nath Seal's Introduction, published in the second volume of this monumental work, which has been accepted universally as the highest authority on the subject even in Europe, furnish convincing evidence of what the Hindu had achieved in the domain of the physical sciences ages before Bacon. But the spiritual genius of the Hindu clearly saw that the real mastery of man over Nature does not lie that way. The root of our serfdom to Nature is not in Nature's strength but in our own weaknesses. It is through our senses that Nature exercises her cruel sway over us. And, consequently, if we could only control these senses, if we could so train our body and our senses that these would be absolutely impervious to the influences of the forces of outer Nature, then we could easily gain a mastery over these outer things which would be permanent and absolute.

This complete mastery has been the aim and objective of all the psycho-physical disciplines of the Hindus of which I have been speaking. The entire system of our yogic discipline has this mastery for its primary end. It is through these disciplines that the Hindu yogee is able to attain that perfect physical state in which neither heat nor cold can affect him in the least. The ordinary physiological functions of their bodies are, therefore, always under the complete control of these yogees. They can go without both food and drink, as well as without sleep or rest for long periods without suffering any discomfort or ill-health. There are yogees who have so trained their bodies that even the vital functions of the lungs and the heart may be stopped by them at their will, without loss of health or life. Of course the number of such adepts is not very large. Even all our holy men do not attain these physical lordships. Many of them, especially those who follow the way of Love and Faith, do not even care for these powers. But still there are such men even to-day, whose powers in these respects have been seen and testified to by even men with modern scientific education in the country.

A yogee of this type, is a well-known personality in West Bengal. He lives in the sacred town of Baidyanath, on the East Indian Railway. Two well-known medical gentlemen of Calcutta saw him some time back; and they have borne witness unto the wonderful mastery that this Hindu yogee has over all the limbs and organs of his body. He can move all the muscles of his stomach at his will, and clear his bowels by this means, far more completely than can be done by any known purgative. This was actually seen and tested by these medical gentlemen. In the presence of these gentlemen this saintly yogee suspended for a time not only the functions of the lungs but even of the heart, and stayed in this state of suspended animation for a length of time which is inexplicable by modern science.

I do not want you to attach any occult significance to these powers. Indeed, the yogees themselves, when they are true and genuine, strongly condemn any such interpretation or assessment. They look upon these physical or psycho-physical acquisitions not as the end of their culture but only as mere by-products. They do not seek these, they come of themselves. It is, however, with these powers that the first step in the progress of the soul towards real and true salvation, is taken. For if the body and the senses are not so completely brought under control that no change of outer natural conditions shall in the least affect them, how then can you expect to concentrate your mind absolutely in the contemplation of the Supreme ? And it is as a preliminary preparation for the attainment of this concentration, that these physical and psycho-physical disciplines have their real spiritual value. The true end and objective of these psycho-physical disciplines is to acquire a complete detachment of the soul from its physical and physiological habiliments.

IDOLATRY OR IDEO-LATRY.

If the main object of all the socio-religious and psycho-physical regulations and disciplines of Hinduism has always been to train the self to completely detach itself from its accidental, though for the time being organic, connections with its outer physical and physiological habitat; that of all our apparently sensuous and external religious ritualism has been to train the mind to see and seize the Unseen, in and through the seen. The outsider, looking upon these rituals in the light of his own special religious traditions and beliefs, or in that of his narrow generalisations from the study of what he calls Primitive Culture, has frequently characterised and condemned these popular Hindu rituals, as idolatry. He has placed, thus, the Hindu's image-worship, in the same class as what is called by European scholars totemism and animism. These popular rituals have also been denounced from time to time even by our own teachers as ignorant and carnal. They have, admittedly, all the evils of all ceremonialism. They have an undoubted tendency to create a divorce between the form and the spirit of higher religious culture. But yet, it is absolutely untrue and unjust to place this so-called idolatry of India on the same level of intellectual or spiritual evolution as the sacrifices and rituals of the savage man. Those who do so forget that this so-called idolatry of the Hindus came in at a much later stage of the religious evolution of the Hindu people, than that at which the so-called totemism or animism of Primitive Culture is found in history.

And to understand this difference between what is called the idolatry of the Hindus and the idolatry of Primitive Culture, you have simply to observe the particular course of religious evolution in India. You may possibly know that one of your own thinkers, the late Professor Caird, in his Evolution of Religion, mentions the three principal stages of it as (i) Objective,

(ii) Subjective, and (iii) Universal. Personally, I strongly object to these terms, as exceedingly misleading. But this is not the occasion nor the place to enter into that large discussion. I would prefer to name these three phases of the general history and scheme of the evolution of religion, as (i) Perceptive, (ii) Reflective, and (iii) Imaginative. Religion originates with man's contact and conflict with what may best be called his Not-Me. We call this Not-Me, in Sanskrit, *idam*, in contradistinction to the me, or *aham*, as it is called in our language. These are the two primal and universal categories according to Hindu thought. All the universe comes under either the one or the other of these two categories. They are present in consciousness even at the lowest stage of our mental evolution. In the earliest stage, this Not-Me is an object of the senses. Man sees it, hears it, touches it, tastes it, seizes it with his outer senses. The earliest gods everywhere are, therefore, sense-objects. You find evidencc of it as much in your own Old Testament as you do in our own Vedas. You find it in the recorded religious experiences both of Rome and Greece. It is universally acknowledged that the present record of the Old Testament is the product of a later and much advanced redaction, representing a much more advanced stage of the evolution of Hebrew thought than what the original documents referred to. But still there are the clearest possible evidences of what may be called a perceptive God-consciousness both in the Book of Genesis and in the Exodus. All the prominent gods of the Vedas are cognised by the senses. Varuna, like Uranus, is the visible sky-god. The omniscience of Varuna is clearly due to the fact,—cognised by the senses, that the sky above us holds all, overlooks all, enters into all, whether great or small whether far or near. If time and space had permitted I would have cited detailed evidence of this universal perceptive character of early religion. The Prophetic Books of the Old Testament, our own Upanishads, the philosophical interpretations of Greek Mythology, all these represent the reflective stage of religious evolution. It is essentially a protestant and antithetical stage. It is characterised by a universal tendency towards mental and metaphysical abstractions. This antethesis does not however hold the mind of man for long. The intellect becomes restless under the confused conflict between idealities and actualities, between the abstractions of thought and the concrete realities of outer experiences, between the unseen and the seen. It is then that the Religious Imagination steps into the breach and with the help of a superb process of idealisation and spiritualisation commences to work up a reconciliation between the Unseen and the Seen.

In our own Upanishads there are two distinct classes of worship. One of these is called *Byetirekee Upasana.* It means the adoration of the Supreme by the method of exclusion or abstraction. The worshipper here tries to meditate on the Deity by constantly saying,—"He is not this: He is not this." In other words, he tries, to think of God as absolutely different, and standing way, from all that is cognised by the senses or can even be concieved in thought. This is the method of worshipping, if worship it may at all be called, the Nirguna Brahman or the Abstract Universsl. The other method is called *Anvayee Upasana*. It means the adoration of the Supreme not by abstracting Him from sense-realities but by seeking to seize and realised Him in and through these very realities. In this method the text is—"All this phenomenal Universe is filled by Brahman." It is the method of idealisation and spiritualisation. Here the Supreme, though unseen is yet the very *esse* and *posse* of the seen. The eye sees Him not, but yet it sees all that is seen because He is the very Eye of the eye. So with all the other senses. He is the Ear of the ear, the mind of the mind, the Life of life. Himself without the senses, He is yet the very soul and essence of both the senses and their objects. He not only transcends all but is equally immanent in all.

This immanental conception of the absolute forms the very plinth and foundation of the third and the most advanced stage of religious evolution The Religious Imagination characteristic of this stage works upon this philosophy of Divine Immanence. What is ignorantly called the idolatry of the Hindus, belongs not to the primitive perceptive stage, to which the so-called totemism and animism of primitive culture belong, but to the third or the imaginative stage of religious evolution.

It is really not idolatry at all but ideolatry.

In judging of this so-called idolatry of the Hindus we must not forget one very important fact, namely, that this idolatry was introduced after the general philosophy of the Upanishads had permeated the entire thought and culture of the people. The gods and goddesses of present-day Hindu ceremonials are not really Vedic. None of the ancient Vedic gods, neither Indra nor Varuna nor the Heavenly Twins, the Asvinikumars, nor any of the old gods are objects of popular worship now. Though the terms, Durga, Kalee, Sarasvatee, etc., occur in the Vedas, they are not the names of goddesses, not at least of those who are worshipped now under these names. All these gods and goddesses belong not to the Vedas but to the Puranas. And in the Puranas, we have most decidedly the later records of what I have described as the imaginative stage of religious evolution. This is one of the main reasons why these gods and goddesses should be regarded not as idols, but as what may be called 'ideols', not gross material images but refined spiritual imageries.

GODS AND GODDESSES AS SUPERIOR SPIRITUAL BEINGS.

This is one interpretation of this so-called idolatry. There is, however, another and more orthodox interpretation also. According to this interpretation, these gods and goddesses are not mere ideas or imageries but real beings infinitely more spiritual and powerful than the humans and differing from them only in degree and not in kind. These gods belong to another and a higher sphere of being. They can exercise as potent a control over the destinies of men even as men can over those of the lower animal world. They are immortals, but not equal to the Supreme, who rules them as much as He rules mankind. Though much purer than humans, these gods have the same passions and are as much subject to anger and jealousy and other spiritual deficiencies as men and women. Their grace can, therefore, be sought by due offerings. And it is to secure the favour of these superior intelligences for the furtherance of more or less mundane ends that these gods and goddesses are usually worshipped. It is very remarkable, indeed, that in the texts used in the worship of these gods and goddesses very rarely have we any reference to the highest spiritual life. The prayers offered to them mostly for progeny and wealth and honour and victory over one's enmies. This is the usual prayer in the current liturgy for the worship of Kalee, Durga and the other manifestations of Shakti.

I have already told you something of this Shakti Cult. Though many people worship Shakti as a goddess among many gods and goddesses, there are some Shakti worshippers, who interpret Her as Prakriti, and whose

Radha-Krishna.

worship of Shakti belongs altogether to a very different and spiritually higher category. This Shakti, by whatever name called, whether Kalee, or Durga, or Jagaddhatree, or Bhavanee,—and these are only different names of the one and the same Reality, —represents, as I already said in my last letter, the eternally self-differentiated Being of the Absolute. It is the same Reality as the Christian Logos, which was in the beginning with God, and which is God, the very God of God. To these advanced devotees the worship of Shakti is no more idolatrous than is the worship of Christ in Christendom; and if they worship Her through images, so do the Roman Catholics also. Of course, there are Protestants who look upon Roman Catholic Christians as idolaters, and they will, of course, pass the same illumined condemnation upon the Hindu Shakti-worshipper also. I have nothing to say of such criticisms. But those who really understand the inner meaning and truth of the Christian mystery of the Trinity, not as a mere dogma or creed, learnt from the Catechist, but as a matter of personal spiritual experience, will, I think, understand the devout Shakti-worshipper much better than the deists and rationalists, whether of India or Europe.

The Cult of Radha-Krishna stands, possibly, on a yet higher ground. It is very far, indeed, from my wish to start any odious comparison between the worship of Shakti and the worship of Radha-Krishna. Such comparisons are hardly permissible in the ideal and culture of the Hindu. To the Hindu, every form of divine worship is good for those who sincerely pursue it. As all roads led to Rome in ancient Europe, so all worships in Hinduism lead to the Supreme. Sree Krishna says in the Bhagabadgeeta :—

ये यथा मां प्रपद्यन्ते तांस्तयैव भज म्यहम् ।
मम वर्त्तानु वर्त्तन्ते मनुष्याः पार्थ सर्व्वशः ॥

"I bless each worshipper after the manner in which he worships me: mankind, O Partha, in every way pursue my own path."

And again,—

यो यो यां यां तनुं भक्तः श्रद्धयार्चितुमिच्छति ।
तस्य तस्याचलां श्रद्धां तामेव विदधाम्यहम् ॥

"The different devotees who desire to worship different images with faith and devotion, I grant them firm faith in their respective images or symbols."

स तया श्रद्धया युक्तस्तस्याराधनमीहते ।
लभते च ततः कामान् मयैव विहितान् हितान् ॥

"That devotee having served his own particular form with this faith, attains the fruits thereof as ordained by me."

In Hinduism, there is no particularistic emphasis, such as we find in all the credal religions: there is no exclusiveness and absolutism such as characterise both Christianity and Islam. The Hindu's God is the God of all. The Universe is His, and He belongs to the Universe. He is the Indweller in every heart, and from there directs and controls the life and evolution of all, according to their respective inner natures. To quote the Geeta once more :—

ईश्वरः सर्व्वभूतानां हृद्देशेऽर्ज्जुन तिष्ठति ।
भ्रामयन् सर्व्व भूतानि यन्त्रा रूढ़ेन मायया ॥

"Oh Arjuna, the Lord is seated in the heart of all creatures ; and is revolving them as if upon a wheel, with His Maya." This Maya is Prakriti. It is really the Law of Being of different objects and persons. It is the specific law of individual life and evolution. And the particularities of the religious life and ordinances of each individual are really determined by their individual law of being. This is the real dharma of each individual. This is his own special religion or law. This is what the Geeta calls—स्वधर्म्मः svadharma. And it is in reference to this special and specific personal law of being, which constitutes the inner individuality and personality of different humans, that Sree Krishna declared in the Geeta that it is far more preferable even to die in the pursuit of this law or dharma than to seek the easier or even the higher law of another person. And in view of this universality of Hinduism, no worship or culture can be condemned. His or her own law or dharma, the disciplines and worships suited to his or her inner nature, is the best for every man or woman. But yet when viewed from the standpoint of the whole or the universal, there are distinctions of superior and inferior between one form and another. This claim to superiority is not individualistic or sectarian but universal.

THE KRISHNA-CULT.

And it is from this universal standpoint that I say that the Krishna Cult stands upon a much higher ground spiritually and philosophically than the other Hindu cults. In the first place, we have here a much firmer grasp of the Philosophy of the Absolute than in any other Hindu system. Krishna is not the Undifferentiated Absolute, so familiar to the student of the popular Monism associated with the name of Samkara. He is not the Brahman of the earlier Upanishads. He is not something like the Pure Being of your own Hegelians, which, as Hegel himself said, is equal to Pure Nothing. This is the Absolute, of which our own Upanishads declared, that they could posit neither being nor non-being. We cannot say that It is, we cannot say that It is not. This Brahman of the Upanishads, the worshippers of Sree Krishna say, is only an effulgence of the Body of Krishna. Brahman is, in other words, only an aspect of the Reality, but not the fullness thereof. That Full Reality is Sree Krishna.

Krishna is a Person, or rather, more correctly speaking, He is the One and the Only Person in the universe. The human personalities are only a faint and distant shadow of His Divine Personality. And He eternally realises His Divine and Absolute Personality through an eternal process of self-differentiation. I have tried to explain briefly what this self-differentiation means in a previous letter, and will not, therefore, repeat that explanation here. This process of the eternal self-differentiation of the Absolute is called in our literature नित्यलीला—nitya leela, or the eternal sport of the Lord. And in this Divine Leela, Radha is the Eternal Partner of Sree Krishna. Radha is the Eternally-Differentiated Self of Sree Krishna. Radha is, therefore, neither absolutely different from, nor absolutely indentical with Krishna. Their mutual relation is one of "inconceivable difference in identity and identity in difference." It is called in Sanskrit अचिन्त्यभेदाभेद. Both this differentiation and this identification are moments in the eternal process of Reason and Love. And it is in and through this eternal process of self-differentiation that Krishna or the Absolute—the परमतत्त्व—the Supreme Reality as He is called in our literature, realises His Personality and becomes The Person. And in this eternal process of Reason and Love, in the very Being of the Absolute, Radha as the momentarily differentiated Self of the Absolute, is also Herself a Person. And it is in and through the Personality of Radha that Krishna reaches and realises His own Personality. Apart from Radha, Krishna is only Pure Being, as the Hegelians would perhaps say. And Pure Being is truly Pure Nothing. It is the Nirguna Brahman or the Abstract Universal of our own Upanishads.

There is, as I already pointed out in a previous letter, very close affinity between the fundamental philosophy of Christianity and that of the Krishna Cult of India. What Christ is in Christian Dogma, that is Radha in our Vaishnavism. There is, however, a very fundamental difference between Christianity and Vaishnavism, in regard to the actual constitution of their respective Deity. Krishna does not stand for Christ, but for the Father of the Christian Trinity. Krishna is the Absolute, but not the Absolute of metaphysical abstraction. He is the Eternally-Self-Differentiated Absolute, realising His Personality through this Eternal Self-Differentiation. The Father is also the same Absolute, the same Person, realising His Personality through the same eternal method of Self-Differentiation. But notwithstanding all this, the Father of the Christian Trinity is only One of the Three Persons of that Trinity, and not the Whole Trinity. In Vaishnavic consciousness Krishna is not a part, not a moment, not an aspect of the Absolute, but the Absolute Itself—Eternally Self-Realised. Krishna is Bhagavan, the Absolute Person. He is, what in our modern phraseology would perhaps be called, the Concrete Universal. We seem to miss somewhat this concrete character in the Father of the Christian Trinity. The Concrete Universal in Christian consciousness is not the Father but the Son, not God but Christ. In our Vaishnavism, it is Krishna who is the Concrete Universal, and not Radha.

And it is this concrete conception of Krishna which fundamentally differentiates our Krishna Cult from Christianity. There is not even the suspicion of any *form* in the Father of the Christian Trinity. The Hindu Vaishnavas openly attribute *form* to Sree Krishna. It is, of course, not a physical form. The form of Sree Krishna in Vaishnavic art is not real but only symbolic. So is also the form of Radha. Truly speaking, neither Krishna nor Radha has any such material and sensuous form. Pure spiritual emotions, we are repeatedly told in Vaishnavic teachings, are the constituents of the Body of Radha. It is a spiritual body, realised in the spirit of the devotee, in his own inner and enlightened emotions, and not something carnal that can be cognised by the outer senses. So also is the Body of Sree Krishna. It is spiritual, and not material, rational and not physical.

What this spiritual *form* of Sree Krishna is, it is impossible for those who are not highly advanced in Vaishnavic culture, to think or imagine. It is revealed not to the outer eye, but in deep trance, in moments of great spiritual exaltation, when the outer senses having been absolutely quieted down, and the inner spiritual faculties having, thereby, been completely freed from all sensuous contacts and impulses, the soul sees with its own refined organs its own Lord and Lover. The experience is absolutely supersensuous and spiritual. But when the mind comes back to itself, at the close of the beatific vision, and is thus related once more to the outer world of sense-forms and sense-sounds, it recalls the inner spiritual experience, by associating it with outer things that represent and resemble it most closely. It is these outer remembrances that create the symbolic forms not only of Sree Krishna but also of all the numerous spiritual beings that are worshipped by the Hindus. These outer forms, visible to the natural eye, are not the real *forms* of the divine beings, but are only something purely mnemonic of their inner spiritual presence. Even so it is with the usual figures of Sree Krishna. This is purely mnemonic. You and I see in these only physical colours and contours; but not having had any previous spiritual experience, we cannot naturally realise their real spiritual significance.

Sree Chaitanya Mahaprabhu, the Avatar of Nadeeya or Navadveepa (Sixteenth Century), in his discussion with Prakasananda, the well-known Vedantin of Benares, declared:—

> ब्रम्ह शव्द मुख्य अर्थे कहे भगवान,
> चिदैश्वर्य परिपूर्ण, अनर्द्ध समान ।
> तांहार बिभूति देह सब चिदाकार,
> चिद्विभूति आच्छादिया कहे निराकार ।

"The specific meaning of Brahman is Bhagavan, who is possessed of absolute spiritual powers, and has neither equal nor superior. His manifestations and His Body are all of spiritual form; ignoring these spiritual forms and manifestations, they call Him formless."

THE "FORM" OF KRISHNA.

You will see from this that the forms which the Hindus attribute to the Supreme are not so gross or material as these naturally appear to the uninitiated stranger. It appears so even to many of our own people, who have not had the profound spiritual training and experiences of the saint and the devotee. There is no suspicion of any gross materialistic conception in regard to the Absolute in our Upanishads. Yet these very Upanishads speak of the Absolute as having what may be called the quintessence of the quality of the different senses, though without the sense-organs. He has no eye, but has the very quintessence of the quality of vision; no ear but the very quintessence of the quality of audition; no olfactory organ, but the very quintessence of the quality of smelling; and so also in regard to all the other senses. This seems to me to be the real meaning of the text:—

सर्व्वेन्द्रिय गुणाभासं सर्व्वेन्द्रिय विवर्ज्जितम् ।

And the irresistible logic of thought that drove Hindu speculations to posit this sense-quality, without the sense-organs, in the Supreme, seems to have been this: When you say that God knows all, the question arises, does He or does He not know all our sense-experiences? If He does, how is it possible, unless He has, not the outer physical senses, but something that possess the essential quality of these organs? In other words, omniscience cannot be attributed to the Deity without positing a sensorium in His Own Being. At least it is impossible to accept His omniscience, in any system of Natural Theology, except upon the hypothesis that God has a sensorium. It is really the sensorium which is of "the quintessence of the quality of the senses." And if you grant a sensorium to the Supreme, you must also grant Him an adequate object for it. In other words, you must grant One Subject and One Object, One Enjoyer and One Object to enjoy, One Will and One Object upon which that Will eternally operates, in the very Being of the upreme, as part of His Unity. And both these,—the Subject and the Object, the Enjoyer and the Enjoyed, the Worker and the Worked, both these terms of these correlations must be coequal and co-existent, co-infinite and co-eternal. This, at least, is how the Hindu Vaishnava must have evidently speculated, when he conceived Sree Krishna as not absolutely "formless" but possessing only "spiritual forms." In the Ultimate Reality, as seized by Vaishnavic experience,—in the Parama-Tattva as it is called,—Krishna is the Subject, Radha the Object. Radha is not absolutely separated from Krishna; nor are the two absolutely united. There is perpetual union and separation between them. As soon as the two are united they separate; and as soon as they are separated, they unite. And out of this endless play of separation and union, flows all the various emotional moods and experiences which constitute the very soul and essence of the highest beatific enjoyments of the Vaishnava devotees. It is because of this Mystery of the Krishna-Radha relation; that the deepest Vaishnavic experience calls Krishna–Akhilarasamritamoorti—

अखिलरसामृत मूर्त्तिः the body of all the rasas, and all amrita,—the body, that is, of all the emotions and all the beatitudes. Krishna is also called Sachchidanandabigraha—सच्चिदा-नन्द विग्रह, which may be rendered into English as the Form of Truth, Intelligence, and Bliss. And all these clearly indicate that whether we are able to understand and realise these mysteries or not, the religion of the Hindu is, after all, not at all so gross as ignorant and unimaginative strangers from Europe or America so often try to make it out. There are deep mysteries here, just as you have in the dogmas and doctrines of Christianity: and if these mysteries of Christianity do not make that religion gross and superstitious: why should the mysteries of Hinduism make it so?

The profoundest significance of Vaishnavism or the Cult of SreeKrishno, lies, however, in its intense and most pronounced note of humanity. In some sense, it may perhaps be said, that of all the Hindu deities, Sree Krishna is the least supernatural. Of course there are numerous manifestations of Sree Krishna, called his avatars or incarnations ; and some of these are non-human, or a combination of the human and the non-human. But these are his descent or avatar in the process of either cosmic or historic evolution. The cosmic character of his incarnation, or more correctly speaking, descent—for that is the true English rendering of the Sanskrit term avatar—is manifest in the earlier forms of the Fish, the Tortoise, and the Boar, which Sree Krishna is said to have assumed. His manifestation as Nrisinha, or the Man-Lion, has also an evident cosmic meaning. But all his later manifestations, as Rama, during the Ramayana Epoch, or as Sree Krishna during the Mahabharata Epoch, all these are distinct human manifestations. Indeed, the Vaishnavas believe that the real and permanent "form" of Sree Krishna is the Divine-Human form. His own "form" is the very spiritual prototype of the perfected human figure. The constituent elements of it are spiritual, and not carnal. But the type is human.

In our highest emotional experiences, especially in our experiences of love, when it "passes beyond the individual and lose itself in the Infinite", do we contemplate and enjoy mere flesh ? Or rather on the contrary do we not feel and realise that the form of the beloved alone is there present in our spiritual vision, but not at all his or her flesh ? In these moments of ecstatic love, the carnal melts imperceptibly into the spiritual, the mere human into the divine. Those who have these experiences, and believe that our love in its highest form is something essentially divine, will perhaps find it somewhat easy to appreciate and enter into the spirit of the high Vaishnavic conception of the real rupa or form of Sree Krishna. Now, this word rupa in Sanskrit is very significant. It is but very imperfectly rendered by the English word form. Rupa does not convey any idea of dimensions as the word form in English does. The spirit has no dimensions, but it has rupa. Rupa means really expression. Our emotions have no dimensions but only expressions or rupas. When, therefore, the Vaishnava speaks of the "form" of his Lord, he does not mean by the term any material concept whatever. No Hindu, really, cherishes such gross notions about his Deity or about any Deity whatever. The soul of man is not material, but a spiritual substance. Yet whenever we individualise this soul, and speak of it as that of John or Martha, of Rama or Lachmee, we attribute some note, or mark, something by which one soul may be distinguished from another. Are these marks and notes physical or non-physical ? If you say they are physical, then either there is no such thing as soul at all or that after death when this physical limitation is removed, there remains absolutely nothing by which one soul can be distinguished from another. But if you accept both the existence of what is called the soul and its immortality, then you must accept this also that this soul has form or, more correctly speaking, a rupa of its own, which is not carnal or physical, but spiritual. It is this spiritual rupa or form which distinguishes one soul from another in the spirit-world, when at death, all their bodily characters are destroyed. And if this is admitted,—and I do not see, my child, how one can avoid this consistently with one's faith in soul and immortality,—in the sense of the continuation after death of the human individuality,—then, it will also have to be conceded as perfectly reasonable, even where one may find it hard to conceive it,—that the Supreme too may have a form or rupa of His Own. Of course the question does not arise with those who do not believe in a Personal Godhead. To the School of Absolute Monism, to those who accept only the Nirguna Brahman as true, and dismiss the Saguna Brahman as unreal and illusory,—those who worship—if worship it may at all be called—the Nirguna or the Abstract Universal only, to them there is no need of positing any such "form" in the Absolute. These do not believe in a real Personal God. The Hindu Vaishnava believes in the Personality of the Absolute. And, consequently, he cannot help believing that the Deity has a form or rupa of His Own. For the very idea of personality involves distinction and differentiation. The differentiation may not be abiding and absolute. In fact neither in our experiences of our own personality nor in our conception of the Divine Personality, is there any such abiding and absolute differentiation or duality. Every differentiation is followed immediately by integration; every duality, immediately it is established, is subsumed in a higher and more perfected unity. So the differentiation and duality absolutely necessary for the Personality of the Godhead is not abiding and absolute but only a mere moment in the Divine Consciousness and Being. But still it is there. It is real, and not illusory. If this differentiation be not real, then the Personality of the Godhead must also of necessity be itself unreal and illusory, mere mayic not paramarthic. The Hindu School of Absolute Monism actually hold this very view of the Personality of God. They regard it as due to Maya. Isvara, the Personal God of the Samkara Vedanta, is, therefore, mere mayic, as much as this phenomenal world. And in the highest state of beatitude this Isvara passes out, like all other dualities and illusions, and the consciousness of the One-without-a-Second, of the undifferentiated Unity alone remains. If you are a Monist of this class, if all your worships and prayers are mere spiritual disciplines of the same class fundamentally as your baths and ablutions, that is,—are only means to an end and not an end unto themselves,—if you believe that when the spirit is purified by these means, and the understanding is finally able to rest in the sense of the Unity, there will be no need for these lower and kindergarten cultures, then you may well and legitimately dismiss the Vaishnavic conception of the eternal and abiding rupa or form of the Supreme as false and fanciful. But not otherwise, my child. At the end, when you have reached the final beatitudes, will your personality be merged in the Being of the Absolute ? Or, will it remain differentiated from Him as now, —differentiated in being only, but united in love and will ? Is love of God a privilege of the saved as it is the duty of those who are in bondage of the flesh and the world ? If so, how will they love and serve the Lord from eternity to eternity, unless there are notes and marks that differentiate the Lord from his servants and devotees? These are queries that cannot be summarily set aside by those who desire to be truly rational and consistent in their faiths and practices.

The Vaishnava Hindu did not brush these aside. He boldly faced them. And realising the imperious necessity of Reason to posit a rupa or form in the Divine to justify His Personality, he unhesitatingly declared that the Deity is not without rupa or form, but that He has a specific Rupa or Form of His Own. It is not a carnal rupa, not a material form, not a form that has dimensions, nor a rupa that has physical colours and contours, but a pure, an invisible, an immaterial rupa or form. His rupa is spiritual. His form is of the elements of Pure Reason.

And we have the nearest approach to Divine Rupa in the rupa of the perfected human. But you will find it exceedingly difficult to clearly realise what the perfected human form is, without previously understanding the Hindu philosophy of what are called the three gunas. These three gunas are the very constituent elements of the universe. All that is, whether living or non-living, whether what we call material or what we call spiritual,—is really a permutation and combination of these. According to the Sankhya System of Philosophy, Nature or the Pradhana as it is called, in its unmanifested state, prior to the beginning of creation, is only a condition of the equillibrium of these gunas. It is only when this equillibrium is disturbed that the process of cosmic evolution starts. Hence whatever is in the universe has these three gunas or properties, in certain permutations and combinations. The analysis, by means of which the Hindu mind arrived at these three gunas or properties as the root-elements of the universe, is not physical but psychological. The gunas are, therefore, not properties of matter but those of mind. They even exist in a state of perfect equillibrium in the very Being of the Supreme, according to Vaishnavic Philosophy, when at dissolution or pralaya, creation is merged in the creator. At the beginning of the next creative process, these once more break out into differentiation, and their equillibrium is lost.

These three qualities are,—Sattva, Rajas, and Tamas. Sattva is the quality of Illumination and Godness. It is the true spiritual quality. Rajas is the quality of Desire and Activity. Tamas is the quality of Ignorance and Inertia. These are variously present in all. Even the gods are controlled by these three qualities. Sattva, you will see, is essentially the highest spiritual quality. Rajas is essentially a mental or intellectual quality. Tamas is a gross animal quality. An excess of Tamas over both Rajas and Sattva, means ignorance and inertia, mere animalism and verminousity. An excess of Rajas in the composition of any person means inordinate desire for enjoyment and possession, and constant conflicts between rivals and competitors for these. An excess of Sattva in the composition of any one indicates his superior spirituality. Such a person is always self-illumined and self-collected, free from all the angry passions that characterise the two lower classes, lives in a perpetual consciousness of the Spiritual and the Universal. His body is perfectly attuned to the highest laws of love and bliss, and his whole being is perfectly attuned to the very Being of the Supreme. In the highest stage of the development of Sattva or the quality of Illumination and Godness, the man becomes absolutely possessed by his God. His body becomes, so to say, the very expression of the pure spiritual energy of the Divine. Having been purified by the psycho-physical cultures of which I have already spoken, his body loses all its animalities, and becomes a perfect instrument for the expression of Divine energy. His mind becomes a perfect receiver and transmitter of Divine Thought, his heart of the Divine Emotions, and his will of the Will of God. Thus perfected, the human becomes divine, the individual becomes the universal. In such a man we see, even with our eyes, that which the eye cannot truly see, and realise with our intellect what transcends the intellectual. It is these men and women whose Rajas and Tamas have been absolutely overwhelmed by the excess of the quality of Sattva, who give us a glimpse of what we see, in moments of the most exalted beatitudes, as human perfection. It is this perfected human who slightly reveals what the Vaishnava worships as the Rupa or Form of his Lord.

We have, thus, in the higher thoughts and ideals of the Krishna

Cult in India, a strange apotheosis of the human, such as is not found perhaps in any other religion. Of course, I do not forget that higher Christianity has also tried to do this to some extent. But while the utmost that Christianity has done has been simply to apotheosise the spiritual in man, Vashnavism has sought to apotheosise even the physical in him. All flesh is evil, said Latin Christianity. All flesh is illusory, said Hindu Vedantism. In both Latin Christianity and Hindu Vedantism, we have, therefore, an attempt to repress the natural instincts and appetites of man in the name and interests of the higher, spiritual life. But Vaishnavism has been peculiarly free from these monkish mediævalisms. In both mediæval Hinduism and mediæval Christianity social life and relations and man's general sense-activities are only tolerated, but never whole-heartedly encouraged. Vaishnavism has been able to do this; because of the way in which it has from of old, persistently sought to idealise and spiritualise the senses, and all the human affections and relations. Vaishnavism has been able, therefore, to avoid both mediæval monasticism, and modern materialism. It condemns equally the repression of the senses and affections of man, as well as their Godless and lustful service. Its aim is not mere regulation of the senses, but their idealisation and spiritualisation. To the truly pious Vaishnava his body is not his own, but that of his Lord Sree Krishna. The service of his body, therefore, is really service of Krishna himself. His care and regard for his own flesh is of the same character as his care for the image of his Krishna, and he seeks to cultivate the same sacred sentiments in relation to the daily service of his own physical body, as those with which he worships his Deity, through his special symbol. I know of Vaishnavas who are literally lost in beatific exaltation when dressing after their daily ablutions, at the thought that the image of their own body upon the mirror before them, is really the very instrument of the leela or sport of their Lord.

This leela or sport of Sree Krishna has two aspects : one inner and the other outer. The inner leela, called in Sanskrit, antaranga leela, is the eternal sport of the Lord within His Own Being. Radha, His Own self-differentiated Prakriti, is Krishna's Partner in this inner or antaranga leela. This inner or antaranga leela stands outside the time series. It is eternal. It is also called in our literature, aprakrita leela, or Supranatural sport. There is, however, another aspect of the leela of the Lord. It is his outer leela, called also His prakrita or natural leela. In Sanskrit it is also called His bahiranga leela. Bahiranga means the outer body. This Universe is the Outer Body of Sree Krishna. This is what is called his

Visvarupa or Universe-Form. It was this Universe-Form of the Lord which was revealed to Arjuna at the field of Kurukshetra, of which we read in the Geeta. The bahiranga leela of the Lord means, therefore, his leela or sportive manifestation in the outer cosmic life and activities, and especially in the human kingdom. This outer or bahiranga leela is not an absolute necessity of His Being. That inner necessity is fully met by His inner leela of which Sree Radha is His Co-Partner. As the Co-Partner of the Lord in His inner or antaranga leela, Sree Radha is a necessity of the very Being of the Absolute. Without Radha He is incomplete, unconscious and inactive,—mere Nirguna Brahman, or the Abstract Universal. Sree Krishna cannot exist without Sree Radha, just as in Christian consciousness the Father cannot exist without the Son, God without Christ. Purusha and Prakriti, Krishna and Radha, Father and the

Son, God and Christ,—cannot exist without one another, The One, without the Other is unreal, a mere abstraction. But the same necessity does not exist in regard to the bahiranga or the outer cosmic leela or sport. The Absolute is full and complete in His Own Being. This outer phenomenal world is not at all a necessity of His Being. This is the common Vaishnavic and Christian view. The world is not necessary for God. But He is necessary for the world. He has no need, really, of us: we alone have need of Him. Our relations with Him are not necessary like those of Radha in Vaishnavic consciousness, or of Christ in Christian consciousness. In Christianity Humanity is God's, not upon its own right, but through Christ. Mankind are sons of God, not on their own right but, through adoption, in Christ. Similarly in Vaishnavic consciousness, the jeeva—the common name for all intelligent creation, including both human and non-human,—is Krishna's, not upon the jeeva's own right, but through His Prakriti, by adoption. We are not, according to real Hindu Theism, as distinguished from Hindu Monism of the Samkara-Vedanta School,—the image of God, but that of His Prakriti. Not Krishna, but Radha is our prototype. We are not Purushas, but Prakritis. Purusha is One: and though His specific Prakriti also is One, yet there are an infinity of inferior prakritis. Radha is Krishna's Own Real Superior Prakriti: we humans are also His superior or para-prakritis, but only by adoption so to say, through Radha. As in His Own Inner Being, Krishna is eternally engaged in His inner or antaranga leela with Radha as His Co-Partner, so in this outer cosmic leela we humans are the co-partners of the leela of the Lord. Our bodies and our senses are the instruments and vehicles of His leela or sport. The purification of the body means, thus, the brightening of the instruments of the leela or sport of Krishna. Krishna enjoys this world of senses in and through our senses. The due cultivation of the sense-life is, therefore, the service not of the senses, but of Krishna Himself. One of the definitions of Bhakti or love of the Lord in Vaishnavism is, therefore, this, namely, that it is the service of the Director of the senses with the senses themselves. Krishna as the Indweller is the Director of all our sense-activities. His service, through the sense-activities is, therefore, a service of love.

But as long as we have a sense of ownership over our own body and our senses, so long Sree Krishna cannot use and enjoy these as the instruments and vehicles of His own leela or sport. His leela or sport, whether in His Own inner Being or in this outer creation, whether it be antaranga or bahiranga, is always with Sree Radha, and not with any other being. Before our bodies and our senses can be used by Sree Krishna as instruments and vehicles of His leela, they must cease to be ours, and become absolutely Radha's. We must cherish absolutely no sense of proprietorship over these. This sense of ownness over one's body and the senses is, according to Vaishnavic ideals, the greatest of all sins. To deny them their legitimate play and fulfilment, to seek to repress their natural activities by cruel penance and monkish renunciations, is also equally sinful. To torture the body under a mistaken ideal of religion and piety is to torture Krishna Himself. To use it for gross and selfish enjoyments is to usurp the very rights and liberties of Sree Krishna Himself. The Vaishnava desirous of cultivating the love of the Lord must carefully avoid both these extremes. This is the negative side of the higher Vaishnavic culture. The positive side consists in the absolute dedication of the body and the senses to the service of Krishna. The senses are not ours but Krishna's, it is He alone who has a right to their use and enjoyment. But He uses them and enjoys them not as our own, but as Sree Radha's. The devotee, in what people call his own sense-life and sense-activities, is merely a blessed witness of the leela or sport of the Lord. It is not the leela between Sree Krishna and himself, but between Sree Krishna and Radha. He sees and enjoys in his own body this Radha-Krishna leela. This is the highest Vaishnava ideal. Our self is not directly the partner of this supreme leela, but simply a witness of it. As in the deepest Christian experience, the Christian devotee is not the direct participant in the transcendental colloquy between the Father and the Son, but is only a witness of it: as the loftiest aspiration of the Christian saint is not to join that eternal colloquy between the Father and the Son, but simply to stand from eternity to eternity by the Throne of Glory and there see the Father in the Son and the Son in the Father, and rapturously listen to their blessed colloquy: even so the highest Vaishnavic ideal is to simply witness this Radha-Krishna leela within and without. In his sense-life he seeks to realise this Radha-Krishna leela. It is thus that he loses the conceit of ownership over these. It is by this means that in higher Vaishnavic culture even the very flesh is purified, spiritualised, idealised, and universalised. It is here that we must seek for the secret of that supreme vicariousness of even the sense-life of our highest Vaishnavic devotees.

But in this higher Vaishnavic culture, not only are the body and the bodily senses spiritualised and universalised, but all the social relations are also equally idealised and universalised. The Vaishnavas seek to realise and enjoy the Supreme as what they call

Nikhilarasa mritamoorti, or the "form" of all the rasas and all amrita. These rasas are the emotions. They are the objects of what is called the æsthetic faculty in European literature and philosophy. The analysis of this faculty in Hindu thought is far more thorough than in European thought. This æsthetic faculty is called in our literature the "ranjinee vritti." It is what may be called the faculty of enjoyment as well as the colouring faculty. Ranjan in Sanskrit means both to enjoy and to colour. And the so-called æsthetic faculty does both in regard to our intellectual life. It gives enjoyment to us, as well as lends colour to all our objects of knowledge. The rasas are the objects of this faculty. These rasas are really the emotions. These according to our literature and philosophy are nine in number. They are :—(i) Sringara : also called the adi or the original rasa. It may be rendered into English by love, but love with a clear sex-reference. It is called the adi or the original rasa because it lies at the very root of creation. (ii) Vira: the word is radically the same as the Latin vir, and means the emotion of courage and valour, that which we feel at the sight of acts of physical bravery. (iii) Karuna: pity and compassion. (iv) Advuta: the sense of wonder. Literally, it means the emotion that is quickened in the presence of something that had never happened before. (v) Hasya: laughter. (vi) Bhayanaka: fear. (vii) Bibhatsa: or the sense of the grotesque. (viii) Raudra or the terrible. (ix) Shanta: or absolute quietude. These are the nine rasas. And the Universal as the Source and Substance of these various emotions, is what the Vaishnavas seek to realise and enjoy as this Nikhilarasamritamoorti. It is as the Universal Source and Substance of all our various emotions that the Vaishnava realises Sree Krishna in the moods and expressions of his own physical and sense life.

But to these nine rasas of Hindu Æsthetics, the Vaishnavas add four more that are distinctly human and social emotions. The nine rasas enumerated above are the common experience of all jeeva. We have them in common with our brother animals in what is called the lower kingdom. But these four specific Vaishnavic rasas are confined absolutely to the human kingdom, and are the results of our social relations. These are:—(i) Dasya, or the emotion of the devoted servant or valet towards his lord and master; (ii) Saukhya, or the complex emotions that find play in our deepest friendships; (iii) Vatsalya, or the parental feeling and (iv) Madhura, or the deep emotions that find play in our conjugal life and the true romance of the man-and-wife relation. Sree Krishna is not only the Source and Substance of the lower rasas that rise through our contact and relations with Nature and the lower animal kingdom, but also of all the emotions that find play in our specific human relations. Krishna, to the Vaishnava, is thus Lord and Friend and Father and Son and Lover and Love. All our human relations are mere reflex of these relations that exist in Sree Krishna Himself as part of His Own Being. Sree Krishna, thus spiritualises all these social relations even as He spiritualises our physical activities and enjoyments. In his master the devout Vaishnava, thus sees his Krishna. In his personal friend he realises and relishes Krishna as Friend. In his son and father, in his daughter or mother, he realises and serves his Krishna. In his conjugal life and relation he realises and enjoys the highest, the depest love of Krishna.

It is thus that in Hindu Vaishnavism, we have a more thorough, more concrete, at once a more real and a more ideal presentation of the Universal than perhaps we have in any other culture. In Vaishnavism the innate sense of the Spiritual and the Universal of the

Indo-Aryan Race-Consciousness seems to have found its loftiest and deepest expression.

If, my child, you want to visualise the Soul of India you must seek and find it in

Sree Krishna.

PART II.

SOME WORLD PROBLEMS.

THROUGH

INDIAN SPECS.

SOME WORLD PROBLEMS.

RACE-EQUALITY.

Are all races of men equal? The question raises another: Are all men equal?

The Church and the State had both combined to set up various artificial barriers in Europe, in the middle ages, against individual effort and initiative, denying to the laity and the general masses of people the privileges and opportunities enjoyed by the clergy and the classes. The dogma of human equality preached by the Eighteenth Century Illumination, was only a protest against these artificial distinctions. These distinctions were based upon an exaggerated theory of human inequality. The protest against this theory was an equally exaggerated statement of human equality.

All men are equal, declared the authors of the American Constitution. But are all men equal? Is it a statement of fact? No one would say it is. All men are not equal: rather that is the truth. Some are strong, some weak, constitutionally: some intelligent and some dull, from congenital causes: some endowed with exceptional aptitudes for a perfect moral life, some cursed with inherited criminal instincts. These inequalities exist everywhere, and are absolutely undeniable. The principle of human equality must, therefore, be interpreted in some other way.

The fact is that the democratic gospel of human equality means, really, not equality of endowments or acquisitions, but simply the right of every individual, whatever his birth or social position, to have equal opportunities with other individuals, to freely pursue and realise his personal end and destiny, absolutely unhampered by any restrictions or limitations whatever, except such as his own capacities and acquisitions may themselves impose.

Equality does not even mean equality of rights. No person can have a right to any position or privilege the duties of which he may not be able to adequately discharge. Children have the franchise nowhere, and no one would contend the deprivation to be an injustice. Rights are determined by duties, and duties by capacities. Owing to unequal capacities, there can really be no equality of rights.

Rationally interpreted, equality can mean, therefore, only one thing, namely, equal claim to the opportunities of life. In other words, the dogma of equality demands that no individual or class or caste shall be prejudged and prejudiced in regard to their capacities or incapacities owing to the accidents of birth, but that every individual shall have the freest scope for proving what he or she may be worth, as a social asset, shall be allowed to test for himself or herself their personal endowments and capacities, and to claim and enjoy the social and political rights to which their endowments and capacities might entitle them.

All men are equal means only this, namely, all men are entitled to have equal opportunities, and nothing else.

But this question of equal opportunities raises another. Opportunities are only for those who can utilise them. Why should the stronger or the more capable offer equal opportunities to the weaker or the less capable, which would involve much dissipation of energy and woful waste of time, and the creation of future rivals and competitors in the race of life. The question cannot be satisfactorily answered by any purely individualistic social philosophy.

The French Revolution started the cry of Liberty, Equality and Fraternity; but it did not fully realise the organic unity existing between them. Equality necessarily followed Liberty. There is no Liberty without Equality, as Fichte declared. This much the French Revolution clearly understood. Liberty and Equality formed, therefore, an organic whole, the one demanding the other as a logical necessity. But pure individualism has no such necessary relation to Fraternity. Fraternity is the formula of Association; and the Principle of Association is very feebly grasped by the individualistic philosophy upon which the gospel of the French Revolution was essentially based. Fraternity, in this gospel, was, therefore, either only another name for human equality, or a mere generous sentiment that had no organic relation to the philosophy of that epoch-making movement in Europe. The dogma of human Brotherhood of the French Illumination which still holds sway over European thought and philanthrophy, was simply the expression of a broad human sympathy, and not the statement of a fundamental truth of social philosophy. Claiming freedom for themselves as the highest good, they wanted it also for others: this was the underlying meaning of the gospel of human brotherhood preached by the authors of the French Revolution. This sympathy was perhaps prompted very largely by their intense hatred of the royalty and the aristocracy in general. Mazzini was among the first to recognise the lack of philosophical basis of the dogma of Fraternity as propounded by the French Revolution. "Fraternity does not supply," he said, "any general social terrestrial aim; it does not even imply the necessity of an aim. It has no essential and inevitable relation with a purpose or intent calculated to harmonise the sum of human faculties and forces." And he pointed out that fraternity, though a necessary link between the terms liberty and equality, which sum up the individual synthesis —does not pass beyond that synthesis: that its action is limited to the action of individual upon individual, that it might be denominated charity, and that though it may constitute a starting point whence humanity advances in search of a social synthesis, it may not be substituted for that synthesis.

The humanitarianism of the French Illumination, upon which the dogma of human brotherhood is based, was really more sentimental than rational. Philosophical humanitarianism can only grow from a clear and strong conception of Humanity as an organic whole. Modern thought in Europe has risen pretty fully to an organic conception of society. The slow growth of this organic conception of society, is seen in the advance of Socialism or Collectivism in every European country. Socialism is as yet a mere economic, or at most a politico-economic theory; and its strong economic emphasis is due to the excessive industrialism of the present age. But the philosophical basis of Socialism or Collectivism is found only in the new conception of society as an organic whole.

And this organic conception of society really supplies the foundations of the doctrine of individual freedom and equality. The claim to equal opportunity, is really set up not by the individual or for the individual, but by Society, for itself,—the realisation of its own ends. If social life were not something organic, that is something which had an end unto itself, if social relations were not something interdependent upon one another and upon the collective life of the community as a whole, if individual self-realisation were possible without the simultaneous furtherance of social ends, if it were possible without the similar self-realisation of the other members of the social whole, human equality would have no ethical significance, and human freedom would kill all altruism, and selfishness instead of self-sacrifice, would be the normal rule of life; struggle for existence and the survival of the fittest would be the law of the human, as it is, to such an extent, the law of the animal kingdom; and liberty would mean not closer unity and stronger amity, but keener discord and wider gulf between man and man.

Collectivism is the real philosophy of Democracy.

Humanitarianism is the fundamental philosophy of Race-Equality.

This Collectivism is an essentially organic conception. The conception of the Whole here is not that of Unity but of Totality, which both sums up and and transcends but does not destroy or ignore, Duality or Differentiation. It is a whole not made up of separate parts, as an arithmetical total, but a living whole, composed of living parts, a whole that cannot live apart from its parts and parts that cannot live apart from the whole. Here the parts find their fulfilment in the whole, and the whole finds its expression only through the parts. The decadence of a part means the partial decadence of the whole, and through the whole, a partial decadence also of the life of the parts.

This Humanitarianism is also an essentially organic conception. In Collectivism, Society is the whole, the individuals are its parts: in Humanitarianism, Humanity is the whole, the races are the parts.

As individual equality does not mean that all men are equally endowed, but only this, namely, that all men have a legitimate claim to equal opportunities of self-development and self-fulfilment, in and through the collective life and activities of the social whole; so racial equality does not mean that the different races are equally, that is uniformly, constituted or endowed, either physically, intellectually, or morally, but only this, namely, that every race, whatever its endowment or actual acquisition, shall have, like every other race, the same unrestricted opportunities of growing to its own highest stature, and realising its own specific life in the collective life of Humanity. Individual equality means freedom of movement and growth, for the realisation of individual ends: Racial equality means the same freedom of movement and growth, for the realisation of racial ends. The one has reference to social wholes, the other to Universal Humanity. Human equality would have no meaning if each individual human unit were not an end unto itself: Racial equality also can have no meaning if each race or nation is not an end unto itself. But specific ends are always subordinate to and dominated by universal or general ends. Individual ends are subordinate to and dominated by general social ends; and similarly, racial ends are subordinate to and must always be dominated by, the universal ends of Humanity. And as in all organic relations, so here also the larger element shall not hinder but on the contrary help the smaller ones; and the higher ends shall not cancel or destroy but rather legitimately advance and fulfil the lower and the subordinate ends.

As an individual or personal end, sufficient unto itself, but organically bound up with universal social ends, constitutes the fudamental basis of individual freedom and equality, so what may be called racial ends, that while sufficient unto themselves, are yet organically bound up with the larger and higher ends of Universal Humanity, constitute the fundamental basis of racial equality. The problem of racial equality must, therefore, be approached from the stand-point of racial differentiation.

The modern social ideal fully recognises individual differentiations, which form really the basis of the human personality. Indeed, it not merely recognises, but deliberately tries to maintain and develop and perfect these individual characteristics. We now fully realise what a serious loss the elimination and obliteration of individual peculiarities would be to the collective life and evolution of society. The ideal of modern pedagogy is, therefore, not to develop any one particular intellectual type, but to seek to discover, and to perfect the constitutional peculiarities of the intellect of every individual student, and by this means to work up a complex and complete culture, representing different types, but all united in a common universal ideal. These differentiations enhance rather than destroy the broad and organic unity of culture. For the Intellect is one, though its moods or modes are many. The Mind is one, though the same Mind expresses and realises itself through multitudinous expressions, each peculiar in itself. This variety constitutes both the beauty and the strength of the intellectual life. The different branches of human culture supplement one another and combine to perfect the ideal unity of Universal Culture. All organic unity is unity in difference; to destroy the note of differentiation is not to develop but only to kill this unity. No educationist destroys, in our time, these individual differentiations in the life of their students but rather helps them to grow in their own way, along their own line, to their highest stature, and thus help to make the intellectual life of the community fuller than what it has hitherto been. So also in the æsthetic or the economic life, the ideal of unity and perfection is sought not through uniformity, where every production is like every other production, but through the development of specific variations and wide divergences, each seeking perfection in its own way and along its own line. Even the religious and ethical ideal also seeks to realise itself through the perfection of different types of piety and character. Here there is no attempt to impose any one particular ideal upon all the varieties of human endowment, human effort, and human movement.

Why, then, should the attempt be made in sociology alone? Why should Asia or Africa be judged by the local standards of England or Germany or France or America? Why should New York be the measure of Cairo, or London the measure of Delhi, or

Rome the measure of Benares, or Berlin the measure of Peking?

No man judges the rose by the standard of the violet or the glorious sun-flower by the measure of the daisy. The lion is never measured by the elephant, nor the rhinoceros by the tiger. Here in the vegetable and animal kingdoms, each species is judged and measured by its own specific standard, and not by that of another species or class. Why should it be different in the case of humanity? The genus homo, like every other genus, includes many species. Or if you take humanity as not a genus but only a species, it includes many classes each different, constitutionally, from the others.

Whether there was, originally, only one pair of Adam and Eve or many pairs, is a futile question. The Book of Origins is hidden from the view of man. Science does not waste its precious time in this vain speculation. It always tries to build all its theories and explanations upon what is actually present before it. And what we see now is that the different races of men differ structurally from one another. How or when these structural differences arose or grew we do not know.

All that can be said of these racial differentiations is that they are original and organic, that we have found these there in the structure of the different races from pre-historic times. These racial differentiations are structural, are observed in the physical and physiological structures of the different races of men. Indeed, these physical and physiological differences constitute the basis of our classification of mankind into different groups, *e. g.*, Caucasian, Mongolian, Negro, etc. These differences in physical structure are universally admitted. Attempts have even been made to regard these physiological differences as indicative of mental and moral differentiations. Whether, and how far, these differences of physical and physiological structure indicate intellectual and moral superiority or inferiority, we do not as yet know. It would be rash, in the present state of our knowledge, to try to deduce any large generalisation in regard to this matter, from the researches of Criminal Anthropology. But apart from the accepted differences of physical structure, whatever these may or may not mean to the intellectual or moral capacities of various races, we know, at least so far as the principal races are concerned, that there are equally marked-out differences between them in what may be called their thought-structure, as well as what may be called their social structure. The thought-structure of a race is found in the structural formation of their language. If anatomy and physiology establish the structural differences existing between different races of men, in regard to their physique; grammar and philology establish the fundamental difference existing between them in their thought. And the structure of their thought indicates the fundamental world-view of the race. There are three elements of thought, (1) subject, (2) object, and (3) predicate. And structural thought-differences are indicated by the difference in the emphasis laid by different languages on one or other of these thought-elements. In some languages, for instance, the emphasis is on the subject, in some on the object, while in a few primitive languages it is neither on the subject, nor on the object, but rather on the predicate. It is well known that the construction "I am", indicating mere existence, simple being, without any reference to modes of action, is only possible in the Indo-European group of languages,—in Sanskrit, Latin and Greek and the languages that are derived from these. It means that the consciousness of the subject or the self, has been an original consciousness with the peoples who have from pre-historic times been using these languages. And we find the same supreme consciousness of the self, of Being, of the Absolute, as an original and regulative idea in all the philosophies and religions, in the arts and literatures of these peoples. Thirdly, there are similar differences between different races in their original social structures: among some people this social structure is essentially democratic, the king among these has always been a peer among peers, as in all the branches of the Indo-European family, whether Romans or Greeks or Hindus, and the system of government has been always constitutional; while among others it has been despotic, the king being the military chief, a law unto himself. There are all these structural differences between the different races of men. In considering the question of race-equality, these fundamental racial differentiations must be fully recognised.

As individual self-realisation, the recognised ethical end for the individual, demands the highest development of his individuality, so racial self-realisation means the highest development of what may be called raciality : the evolution and not the obliteration of race-characteristics. As the highest social end can be reached only through the highest development of individual life and thought, so the highest ends of Humanity can only be attained through the highest development of racial life. And this development is possible only when the different races have the same unrestricted freedom of self-development which is given to every individual in every civilised community. This freedom is given to individuals not merely in their own interest, but in the interest of society, which requires the highest development of its individual members for the realisation of its own life. The freedom of self-development is similarly claimed for individual races of men, not only in their own special interest, but in the larger interests of Universal Humanity, which requires the perfection of the racial types for its own self-realisation.

The individuals are parts, Society is the Whole. The races are similarly parts, Humanity is the Whole. The relation is organic. But in all organic relations, the whole is always involved in its parts. Parts do not partially contain the whole, but they have the wholeness of the whole in themselves. The expression of the whole in the parts is no doubt only partial, but the potentiality of the whole is in the parts in all its completeness. The full and complete ideal of Humanity is present in every race of men. The expression may be more or less, but the potentiality is there in all its completeness. This is the necessary implication of every evolutionary process. The oak is in the acorn, not a mere part of it ; the man is in the human cell, and not a mere portion of him ; so Humanity, as an organic whole, is in every human society, in every racial organisation, and not a mere part of it. Humanity is not a mechanical, but an organic whole. It is, therefore, involved in every individual human being, and equally, in its collective character, it is potentially present in every race of men. It is the regulative idea in the evolution both of individuals as of races.

If Humanity be in every race of men, as the regulative idea in their evolution, then every race-culture must be something that is essentially complete in itself. Some may be advanced, some backward, some more developed, some less, but no race-culture can, then, be without the potentialities of the full and completed ideal. The difference between them can only be, in that case, either a difference in evolution or a difference in emphasis and expression. These differences can only be similar to what is universally observed in every country and community between children and adults, or between one individual and another. No one ever denies the presence of the full potentiality of manhood or womanhood to a boy or a girl; nor do we refuse to admit grown up men and women into the common fellowship of humanity, because they do not represent any one particular type. There are children and adults among races of men also; some races less developed and some more, as well as differences of racial characteristics even among the more developed races, but in all of them there is the Common and Universal Humanity.

THE

PROBLEM OF CIVILISATION.

What is civilisation ?

I finished my last record with Mr. Theorde Roosevelt's royal tour in Europe. But Mr. T. Roosevelt had not yet finished with us. And in justice to him, it must be said that he was never, throughout his itinerary in Europe, so much like himself as he was in London, and specially when he delivered his soul of the burden of responsibility that rests upon the civilised man in regard to barbarism that holds sway still over large portions of the globe, and also in regard to those ancient civilisations that, in the opinion of Mr. Roosevelt, had somehow "gone crooked." He stood here as an inspired apostle and prophet of modern civilisation, He is even more than an apostle, he is the avatar of modern civilisation, calling upon the peoples of Europe and America to pursue their mission of fighting barbarism in every part of the world. He had no sympathy with those who, on sentimental grounds, would leave uncivilised peoples to themselves, working out their own civilisations in their own way, and in accordance with their own traditions and capacities. Like all prophets, Mr. Roosevelt has no patience with those weak-minded men who would not do the right because the doing of it may hurt some people's sensibilities. "It is necessary for all of us," said Mr. Roosevelt, "who have to do with uncivilised peoples, and specially with fanatical peoples, to remember that weakness, timidity, and sentimentality, may cause even more far-reaching harm than violence and injustice." And he urged that "the civilised nations who are conquering for civilisation savage lands, should work together in a spirit of the hearty, mutual good-will."

"Ill-will between civilised nations is bad enough anywhere, but it is peculiarly harmful and contemptible when those actuated by it are engaged in the same task, a task of such far-reaching importance to the future of humanity, the task of subduing the savagery of wild man and wild nature and of bringing abreast of our civilisation, those lands where there is an older civilisation which has somehow gone crooked."

This is the new Rooseveltian evangel. But what is civilisation? and, indeed, what is barbarism either? I think that the only practical definition of these terms is that barbarism is your ism, and civilisation is my isation. I am white; and, consequently, whatever belongs to the white races is naturally to me an emblem of civilisation. You are brown or black or yellow, you are not white; and, consequently, whatever appertains to your thought and life, except that which you have borrowed from me, is an emblem of either barbarism, or at best of an old, worn-out, and effete civilisation,—what was, perhaps, civilisation at one time, but which has, as Roosevelt puts it, somehow gone crooked in our day.

This definition is in perfect accord with ancient practice. The word barbarism is of Greek origin, and, among the Greeks, a barbarian was only a foreigner. And the origin of the term is significant. It is derived, as you, know, from barbarous which literally meant only stammering, and was subsequently applied to mean whatever was foreign, owing to the unfamiliar sound of foreign tongues. The term had thus its origin in ignorance or more correctly speaking in ignorance illuminate with conceit. And the something may, to some extent, be held to be true even to-day. Our characterisation of foreign peoples as barbarous is due to the combined action of our ignorance of them on the one side, and our conceit concerning our own character and culture on the other. The Greek judged the foreigner by his own Grecian standards; we of modern European civilisation do the same, judge Egypt and India, and China, by our own European standards, and because these ancient countries fail to reach our ideal, we, like the Greeks of old, vote them as either barbarous, or at the most, inheritors of an old civilisation that has "gone crooked."

This is the root of the misconception. Foreigners from the colder regions of Europe and America going to India are shocked by the nakedness of her people. They see men going about with nothing except their loin cloths, and women, too, without the kind of dress which is the symbol of decency in their own community; and they are shocked by the sight. The natives of the country seem to the European tourists almost like lower animals. And they naturally put them down as barbarians. I am afraid that the Indian, not brought up in modern English ways, would be equally shocked by many things even in our own glorious civilisation here. He would not understand our exquisitely decent ball-dress, for instance; or appreciate the modesty of our bathing-costume. For obvious reasons, they might not characterise all these as barbarism; but the feeling that originally gave birth to the term, would, all the same, be there. Nor did the Greeks alone, in the ancient world, use to regard the foreigners, as belonging to a lower culture. The Hebrews made a similar distinction between themselves and the Gentiles, a distinction that did not go quite in favour of the character and culture of the latter. The Hindus too, I think, in their own day, made similar distinctions, and applied the not-very-complimentary term Mlechchha, to signify the non-Hindu. And the Mlechchha was always an unclean person, a member of a lower race and an inferior civilisation. The mlechchha, the gentile, the barbarian, these are all of the same class. They all indicate a lower and inferior culture. They all have their origin, oftentimes, in a want of knowledge and appreciation of foreign thought and life. And the old habit persists even to-day, though without the old excuse,—of relegating to a lower position every thing that goes against our familiar thoughts and ideals.

THE DEFINITION OF CIVILISATION.

People talk glibly of civilisation and barbarity, but I am afraid that if they were asked to clearly define these terms, they would find it no easy task. Indeed, though we all talk so much of civilisation, their dictionaries have not as yet a decent definition of the term. Johnson, their greatest lexico-grapher, recognised the difficulty of fixing any clear meaning to the term of civilisation;

and, as Boswell says, would not admit into his folio dictionary.

"On March 23rd (1772) I found him," says Boswell, "busy preparing a fourth edition of his folio dictionary. * * He would not admit civilisation, but only civility. With great deference to him, I thought civilisation from to civilise, in the sense opposed to barbarity, better than civility." And this is the sense in which all the subsequent dictionaries generally interpret the term. But as barbarity originally meant only that which is foreign, and the idea is still hidden in the word, so civilisation really means, to most people, only that which belongs to the general culture of their own race and country or is consonant with their own habits and ideas.

In this sense,—which, indeed, seems to me to be the only real sense in which the term is generally used, every body is entitled to call everybody else uncivilised. People did so in the past, and they are welcome to do so even now. But when this so-called civilisation is claimed by any person or class or country as a justification for interfering with the legitimate rights of self-development and self-fulfilment of other persons, classes or countries, under the plea of advancing universal humanitarian interests, as Mr. Roosevelt distinctly attempts, the thing becomes a bit too serious, and demands a little careful scrutiny.

What then is this civilisation, in the name of which Mr. Roosevelt wants to ride rough-shod over the liberties and sensibilities of non-white races? Of course, in justice to Mr. Roosevelt, it should be said that he does not prescribe such drastic remedies for Japan, and hardly for China, either. The reason of these exceptions is also evident. Japan is too strong to be treated in this fashion; nor would China stand with patience the benign process or accept the gift with gratitude. Mr. Roosevelt would not dare to call

Japan barbarous. Japan *is* civilised, without question. The Western nations who would not admit that Japan was civilised fifteen or twenty years back, have been thoroughly convinced of her civilisation now, through the successful way in which she licked one of the great Powers of Europe both on land and sea, in the last war. This sudden elevation of Japan to the level of modern civilisation, by means of a successful fight with a mighty European Power, would lend a very queer interpretation to the term. Aptitude in military organisation and mastery of the modern weapons of whole-sale slaughter would thus be the surest test of civilisation. Practically it is so. This is the direct implication of the Rooseveltian gospel. If the Hottentot or the Fijian could handle the dreadful engines of modern warfare as cleverly as they wield their old weapons, Mr. Roosevelt would not have dared to urge his fellow Europeans to civilise them even by violent methods if these become necessary, in the interest of humanity.

Nor can we honestly deny that there is an underlying intellectual if not exactly a moral, principle involved in this view. A certain amount of intellectual, and a good deal of material, advancement is absolutely necessary for using these modern implements of war. They are, in the first place, the inventions of mighty intellects. In the next place, the efficient organisation of modern armies would be impossible without even a certain degree of moral advancement of the race. Modern warfare is not a mere display of sheer physical force. In fact in point of physique, the primitive races, or at least some of them, could hardly be regarded as in any way inferior to the European. The main question in modern warfare is not one of muscle but rather of brains. The test that Japan has stood, is not a mere physical test, but is an essentially intellectual and, to some extent, even a moral test. Modern civilisation, therefore, even though Mr. Roosevelt is its apostle, accepts a somewhat higher standard than that of mere brute force.

But is that the highest? That is the question. Professor Leckey in his History of European Morals, gives really the truest estimate, it seems to me, of that civilisation for which Mr. Roosevelt has so boldly stood up among us. Leckey says:—"The entire structure of civilisation is founded upon the belief that it is a good thing to cultivate intellectual and material capacities even at the cost of certain moral evils which we are often able accurately to foresee."

This preference of material to moral and spiritual endsconstitutes, as Leckey points out, a predominant feature of what Mr. Roosevelt calls civilisation. But are we to accept it as the only or even so far as the highest civilisation that humanity has attained or is capable of attaining? When we compare one civilisation with another, or compare civilisation on the one side, and what is called barbarism on the other, we assume, whether consciously or unconsciously, the existence of a common ideal or end between both of these factors of comparison. Without this common ideal no legitimate comparison would be possible. And the question is this, what is this common ideal? Europe has no more right to judge Asia or Africa by its own standard than Asia or Africa has the right of judging Europe by their own standards. Such comparisons might indicate the difference between Europe and Asia or Africa, but mere differences are no evidence of either superiority or inferiority. If Europe claims a superior civilisation to that of Asia or Africa, she will have to submit these claims to a tribunal that stands higher than both the parties. Is there such a tribunal? Is there such a standard? European culture is as much a local thing, as much a particular, as Asiatic or African culture. And particulars can never be compared except in and through the Universal. The Universal in human civilisation must, therefore, necessarily be the only true standard by which different types of civilisation can be judged, and, in the light of which they may be compared, one to the other, and that which is higher reasonably differentiated from that which is lower. Mr. Roosevelt has not, as yet, discovered, or if he has discovered, he has not as yet published to the world, this universal ideal of human culture and civilisation, in the light of which alone he could reasonably adjudge one civilisation as higher and straight, and another as lower and "crooked."

THE TEST OF CIVILISATION.

What, indeed, is the test of civilisation? What is the ideal-end which human culture has always been trying to reach? The ideal, however, is not something that is to be found somewhere outside the real. The real, everywhere and always, suggests the ideal, and nowhere exhausts it. This is the common characteristic of all ideals, whether in nature or in art, whether in the world of matter, or in the kingdom of man. The ideal of the rose does not stand apart from the rose, nor is it exhausted by any particular specimen of the rose. It is that towards which all roses tend, which every rose tries to realise, and which all the roses do partially realise, some more and some less, but which is never absolutely exhausted by any particular rose, whatever may be the stage of perfection that it has been able to reach. A study of the genus rose as a whole in all its varieties and through all its stages of past evolution, can alone reveal to us the real nature of the ideal-end of the evolution of the rose--

plant. Similarly it is not the study of a particular civilisation or even that of a few familiar types of it, that can enable us to discover the ideal-end by which alone can we adjudge the higher and the lower between different human civilisations. European civilisation, at its best and highest, is essentially a mere particular among particulars. It is a local something. It has been influenced more or less by local causes and conditions, physical and physiographical, as well as social and historical. These local conditions and causes have lent a particular colour and trend to this civilisation. The Universal is implied, no doubt, in this particular civilisation as in other particular civilisations, but it is not identical with any of them. And this universal ideal-end of all civilisations must be discovered, before we can get a right standard by which to judge which particular civilisation is higher and which really lower.

THE HISTORIC METHOD.

And the only method of inquiring into this ideal-end of human culture and human civilisation is what is known as the historical method. We must study the course of evolution of human society and the institutes of human civilisation, and from the materials collected through such studies, we must work out our generalisations concerning universal human culture and human civilisation. Such a study of the history of human civilisations, will necessarily reveal certain elements that are common to all civilisations, and what the real meaning and significance of these common elements are. What the Scriptures are to religion, that is history to civilisation. Scriptures are the records of the actual religious experiences of mankind : history is the record of the experiences of men in the matter of civilisation and culture. Indeed, history is a much more large and comprehensive human record than Scriptures.

The Scriptures record only a part of men's experience, history is the record not of a part but really of the whole of a man's experiences. History is a record much of his spiritual as of his secular life, a record equally of his spiritual experiences as of his social and economic struggles. And history, therefore, finds us the key to every department of human activity and human advancement. The history of human civilisation will reveal, therefore, the true character of the ideal-end which it seeks to reach, which is at once both the inspiration and the goal of all its endeavours.

MASTERY OVER NATURE.

And the history of human civilisations discovers the essential elements of these. Here we see how man advanced step by step from the condition of almost pure animals to that of human beings. The story of this advance is, really, the story of the gradual expansion of man's dominion over outer nature. The primitive man is an absolute or almost absolute slave of the forces of Nature about him. His instincts may enable him, as their instincts enable even the lower animals, to evade the natural forces, but he has practically little or no control over these. Civilisation begins with the assertion of man's mastery over outer natural forces. Mastery over physical natureis, thus, a universal test of civilisation. This is universally recognised. Indeed, the superior claims of the Western civilisation over the older civilisations of India, Egypt, or China, is essentially based upon its greater lordship over natural forces. It is the greatest achievement of nineteenth century science. Even all the engines of destruction, by means of which the European or American holds sovereignty over the older races of Asia or Africa, are the fruits of this science. Here Europe and America are unquestionably ahead of Asia and Africa. And so far, therefore, as mastery over outer natnre is considered, and so far as this mastery is an undeniable test of civilisation, it can hardly be denied that the West is decidedly more civilised than the East.

But the question here is, is this mastery over external nature the only or the highest test of civilisation ? That civilisation does not even take its birth unless man establishes some degree of mastery over his natural environments, need not be questioned. We had this mastery in ancient India, as well as in ancient Egypt. They had it in China and other old countries. But to say that every civilisation must establish some mastery over external nature is only to lay down the minimum condition of civilisation. But the minimum condition of the existence of a thing is not absolutely the highest standard of its perfection. Physical health and strength are essential conditions of an ideal manhood or womanhood; but, therefore, it does not follow that the stronger or healthier is a man or woman, he or she is nearer to that ideal. Similarly, because a certain amount of mastery over nature-forces is an essential condition of civilisation, it does not follow that the greater this mastery the higher is any particular civilisation which may possess it. There are other things, that go to the making of the ideal of manhood or womanhood than mere physical health or strength ; so there are other things, besides this mastery over nature-forces,—which is the predominant achievement of modern science,—that go to the making and perfection of civilisation ; and both the ideal man or woman as well as the ideal civilisation must be judged by these other things also, as much as by this elemental condition of mere physical health and strength or mastery over nature-forces, however wide or complete that mastery may be. And the real trouble with those, who like Mr. Roosevelt, claim the highest civilisation for Europe and

America, is that they have little or no appreciation of these other things. It is, therefore, that generalising from the actualities about him. Professor Leckey had to say that the whole structure of civilisation, by which he meant European civilisation, is based upon the belief that it is a good thing to cultivate intellectual and material capacities even at the cost of certain moral evils which we are able accurately to foresee. These intellectual and material capacities really mean those that secure for us a mastery over our natural environments. This mastery is, thus, the European's test of civilisation.

THE MEANING OF NATURE.

This test may even be accepted, I think, in a general way by everybody. The Indian would accept it as a true test, I should think, as much as a European. But there will be perhaps very wide difference of opinion between them, as to the meaning of the term—Nature. The European means by Nature his physical environments, the subject of the physical group of his sciences. The Hindu understands by the term a good deal more. To the Hindu there are really two, and only two, orders in creation : the Aham and the Idam—the Me and the Not-Me, the Self and the Not-Self. Mastery over Nature, which he would gladly accept as a test of civilisation, includes, to his mind, if I have understood him aright, not merely physical nature, but everything and all things that come under the category of the Not-Me or the Not-Self, the category of the Idam,—of "this" or "that" in Sanskrit, as opposed to the Aham or I. In this sense, even his own body, his senses and appetites, are to him not his Self, not his Aham or I or Me, but his Not-Self, his Idam or this or that. Mastery over Nature would thus mean not merely a control over natural forces but over those senses and appetites, through which alone can these natural forces hold and exercise any sway over him. Heat and cold, plesasure and pain, these so-called pairs or opposites, constitute the secret of Nature's hold over man. Because men are subject to these sensations that they are controlled by the elemental forces about them. And they can gain mastery over these elemental forces in a two-fold way : they can prctect themselves against these by restraining and regulating them through their own elemental laws;—that is the way of modern science and Western civilisation ; or they can do so by so training their senses and sensibilities that these elemental forces shall absolutely fail to work on them,—that is the way of psychology or psychophysics, the method so largely in vogue among the ancient and mediæval Hindus. Mastery over Nature was, thus, the common test of civilisation among the Hindus, even as it is among modern Europeans : only the method by which this mastery has been sought by the two peoples has been different ; one has sought it through spiritual the other through physical means. And consequently, a true comparison between the two civilisations would really be a comparison between these two methods,—the spiritual and the physical. Which is higher and which lower ? Which is more effective and which less ?

EUROPEAN AND HINDU CIVILISATION.

Indeed, it seems to me, the fundamental difference between Western European and Eastern Hindu civilisation lies in this, namely, that while the emphasis of the one is on the physical, that of the other is on the spiritual, While, as Leckey points out, the whole structure of Western European civilisation is based upon the belief that it is a good thing to cultivate intellectual and material capacities even at the cost of certain moral evils which we are often able accurately to foresee'; the entire structure of Eastern Hindu civilisation is based upon the contrary belief that it is a good thing to cultivate moral and spiritual capacities even at the cost of certain intellectual and material deficiencies which we are able oftentimes to accurately forecast. So far as I can see this seems to be the fairest presentation of the difference between the two civilisations. And the question is, which, then, is the better and the higher ?

Absolutely speaking, both are evidently partial and defective. The very statement of their respective cases, shows, indeed, their intrinsic limitations. The one seeks intellectual and material good at the expense of the moral. The other seeks moral and spiritual good at the expense of the intellectual and the material. In the ideal civilisation there would be no such partial gain, one department of life would not have to be advanced at the cost of another. The spiritual and the material would each find its own proper place, function, and fulfilment, in a perfected and harmonious whole. There would be no conflict or anthésis between the spiritual and the physical, between the moral and the material, or between the intellectual and the emotional activities and achievements of life. In the light of this ideal, both the Western and the Eastern civilisations are partial and defective. But even as they are, which is higher, comparatively speaking, and which lower? Which is going straight and which has gone "crooked"? All this can only be determined by the value at which we assess intellectual and material capacities as against moral and spiritual good. By those who set a higher value upon intellectual and material capacities than upon moral and spiritual achievements, European civilisation of which Mr. Theodore Roosevelt is the Apostle, would be naturally voted as superior : while to those who set a higher value upon moral and spiritual good, the Eastern civilisation would, perhaps, appeal as better.

THE IDEAL OF CIVILISATION.

But neither of these represents really the highest ideal of civilisation. The ideal-end of civilisation is perfection of man, not merely in his physical and material, but equally also, in his moral and spiritual aspects. It is more, it is the perfection of man as a social unit, as a limb and organ of the social whole. As such, he must fulfil himself in and through the fulfilment of the ideal-end of that Whole. The true definition of civilisation, therefore, seems to be that given by Matthew Arnold—it is "the humanisation of man in Society." It means the realisation of man's highest end and perfection in and through the social life. And while from some points of view, the old Eastern Hindu civilisation might seem to be better than the predominantly materialistic civilisation of modern Europe, its anti-social tendencies have been its most fatal defects. Even modern European civilisation, in so far as it is yet predominantly individualistic, suffers from the same defect, though in a somewhat different way. What is needed by both is a recognition of the organic nature of social life. Added to this, Hindu civilisation needs also the recognition of the material possessions and sense activities as necessary vehicles of the spiritual life, and European civilisation needs a similar recognition of the supremacy of the spiritual life over all material possessions and sense enjoyments. The spirit is the idea, matter and sense are its expression. The relation between the two is necessary and organic. For lack of adequate expression, the Idea necessarily suffers. For lack of Idea, expression festers as a matter of equal necessity. The Ideal lies in the harmony between the two. This harmony, this synthesis, between spirit and matter, between Nature and man, between the individual and society is the supreme need of our age. When we are able to work out this synthesis, the West shall have a more correct and appreciative estimate of the East, and the East will have an equally correct and appreciative estimate of the West. And then, this conflict of civilisations will be cancelled and Mr. Roosevelt and his like, will find their occupation gone.

THE

PROBLEM OF NATIONALITY AND EMPIRE.

CLAIMS OF NATIONALITIES.

A Conference on—The Claims of Nationalities and subject Races, was held in London, in June 1910.

It was an international gathering, in which Finland and Georgia, Poland and Ireland, Egypt and India were all represented by recognised spokesmen of their respective peoples. The differentiation that the organisers made between what had hitherto been known as "subject races" and what they called now dependent nationalities, marked at the very outset a very important advance in the general thought of the European peoples in regard to ancient countries like Egypt or India. In some sense this Conference sounded a counter-blast to Mr. Theodore Roosevelt's gospel of civilisation and the big stick. This is not, of course, the first time that liberal-minded and sympathetic members of the dominant European races have pleaded before their own people for a just and kindly treatment of alien peoples subject to their rule. There is an old organisation in England whose object is to watch over the moral and material interests of what are called the native races in Africa and elsewhere. But this and similar organisations of the kind never seem to have gone to the root of the problem which they have been trying to handle. They never questioned the claims of the dominant European powers to a higher civilisation, upon which they based their moral right to rule the less civilised races of the world. The government of these so-called native races by some civilised European nation has always been accepted as a good thing, both in the interests of these races themselves and in those of humanity at large. European domination over non-European races spells the participation by the latter in a higher civilisation and life. It means the substitution of peace and order for disorder and anarchy, the replacement of the rule of might by the law of right, the progress of the people from savagery to civilisation. This general moral plea had never before been examined, much less seriously questioned. The right of every people, whatever the state of their progress or the character of their culture, to freely live their own life and evolve their own destiny, without any let or hindrance from their stronger, and possibly more advanced neighbours, has never before been boldly asserted. All that the friends of so-called native races tried to do was to try to make their lot a little easy and their yoke a bit light. Their claims to sympathetic rule and humane treatment had, thus, been strongly urged before, but their absolute right to self-government and legitimate freedom of self-fulfilment, had never been recognised. There was an implicit recognition of these fundamental principles in the work of this International Conference on the claims of nationalities and subject races.

RACES AND NATIONALITIES.

At the very outset, this Conference started with a clear differentiation between dependent nationalities like those of Ireland, Poland, Finland, Egypt or India, and what are known usually as subject races. This elementary differentiation is bound to clear up a good deal of confusion that still surrounds the problem of nationalities. There is a very wide difference between a race and a nation. In the first place, territorial unity is an essential condition of nationality, but not of raciali' race may spread over different a tant territories, and occupy various parts of the globe, but a nation must be confined to a definite habitat. A race is essentially a homogeneous thing. It has a special physical structure, a special thought-structure, and a special social structure. This three-fold structural affinity is of the very essence of the race-idea. This structural affinity is observed among the different branches of the great Aryan family. It is equally seen among the different branches of the Mongolian family. It is observed among the different branches of the other races of mankind. A nation is, however, a more complex and heterogeneous thing. More than one race can go to the making of a nation. There is a good deal of racial intermixture in all the developed nationalities of the world. The growth of nationalities indicates a higher stage of social evolution, and a more developed order of social life

to dissipate their untruth. If we want imperialism to be just, we must ourselves be first just to it. All imperialists are not moved by unworthy motives. There are men and women, as thoroughly honest as ourselves, who regard imperialism as beneficial to the best interests of humanity, and who lend their support to it, because of its beneficial or supposed beneficial influences. Professor Hobson pointed out this fact, in explaining the reason why imperialism commanded the allegiance of many honest and really well-meaning people. In so doing he made a fairly correct diagnosis of the case before him. Unfortunately, however, even Professer Hobson did not drive this psychology to its legitimate conclusion. But I am not at all surprised at it; for it is only a true philosophy of nationalism that could have given the learned professor the right key to the solution of the problem that he so clearly raised.

NATION-IDEA AND EMPIRE-IDEA.

The greatest fascination of imperialism is that it makes for the unification of humanity to an extent and upon a measure impossible under any other form of human organisation or association. As nations are larger than tribes, even so empires are larger than nations. Raciality is a higher synthesis than mere tribality. Nationality is a higher synthesis than raciality. And imperialism offers, similarly, a higher synthesis than nationalism. The empire-idea is essentially larger and broader than the nation-idea. It aims at the unification of widely separated territories, of widely divergent interests, of widely different cultures and characters, into one organic whole. As families combine into tribes, each family contributing its peculiar characteristics and possessions to the common life of other families, in and through the unity of the tribe-life ; as at a subsequent social synthesis, tribes combine to form races, which, though divided by space, controlled by different environment, evolving under divergent historical epochs, still pursue a common ideal-end, are moved mainly by a common regulative-idea, and thus make for a larger union of mankind than had been realised before; and as at the next synthesis, different racial units combine to form a larger, more complex, and yet more intimate unity, namely, that of the nation; so the unification of these national units into an imperial organisation or organism is really a higher and larger social synthesis than even what has been attained through the nation-idea. It is impossible to deny, therefore, that the empire-idea is positively larger, grander, nobler than the nation-idea. This is the fundamental truth of the concept empire. The family, the tribe, the race, the nation; these are all old syntheses of social progress. The empire is a later synthesis, though not really a new, modern synthesis. From the family to the tribe, from the tribe to the nation, from the nation to the empire, from the empire to universal federation,—this is the complete scheme of social evolution. And in this ascending social series each antecedent term must be judged and justified by each subsequent term. Families must be judged and justified by their capacity to develop into the larger life of the tribe, tribes must be similarly judged and justified by their capacity to grow into the more complex and variegated life of the nations; nations must be similarly judged and justified by their capacity to combine into the wider life of the empire, and finally empires must be judged and justified by their capacity to work out the universal federation of mankind.

This is the correct rationale of imlarialism. Its claims to the attention and allegiance of mainkind are based esseutially upon its promise to work out a larger unification of humanity than has as yet been realised. But what is the true character of this unification? What is the real nature of the unity that humanity has been progressively seeking through the entire course of social evolution? In the first place, it must be understood that unity is not homogeneity. All organic unity is a unity which does not destroy and deny all differentiations and diversities, but which realises itself in and through not only the maintenance of these diversities and differentiations, but even more fully through their development and perfection. Our conception of unity is essentially different as much from the old pagan as from also the mediæval Christian idea of it. The pagan view was the denial of the legitimate freedom of the units in the interest of unity. The social philosophy of paganism regarded the individual human unit as a mere limb of the body politic, having really no end unto himself apart from the common ends of the State. Christianity was the first to enter a protest against the usurpation of the rights of the individual by the Society or the State in Europe. It was the first to proclaim in Europe the divine right of the human personality, to declare that man was himself an end unto himself. But the right to dominate the individual and usurp his legitimate freedom of self-development and self-fulfilment, which Christianity denied to pagan Society and the pagan State, it gradually set up for the Church in the new philosophy of life which it propounded. The old usurpation of the fundamental rights of the human personality was thus continued by the new Church. This was the logical need of the subsequent Lutheran protest, even as the French Illumination with its gospel of absolute individualism was the logical sequence of the philosophy of Christian Protestantism.

A WAR OF HALF-TRUTHS.

All this was what may be called a war between half-truths. The pagan view of social unity was only half a truth. The Protestant Christian view of it which culminated in the individualism of the French Illumination, was equally only another half-truth. The one denied the organic end of the individual, the other ignored the organic end of society. Neither therefore could really reconcile individuality with social unity, freedom with subjection. And the reason was that neither the old pagan view nor even the subsequent Christian view had a true conception of the nature of organic unity. This conception is the latest contribution made by modern thought and research to social philosophy. The modern conception is that society is an organism, but an organism composed of a number of smaller organisms, that have, as such, necessary ends unto themselves. But these individual ends are so arranged that they are interdependent upon one another and upon the collective ends of the social whole to which they belong. The social unity is thus what the philosophers would call, not unity but really totality, which is a much higher category. It is a federal unity, which means the freedom of the parts in the unity of the whole. In a federal organisation the whole realises itself only and always in and through the perfection, each in its own way, of its parts, and these different parts also reach out to and realise their own specific ends in and through the general life and progress of the whole. This is the very essence of the concept organism As society is an organism this must be the universal law and condition of social progress and the realisation of social unity. For society to usurp the legitimate freedom of movement and development of the individual, is to commit suicide. For the individual to seek his own individual end without regard for the larger collective ends of society, is to miss that very end itself. This is the modern conception of the social ideal.

It is a fundamental social conception. It is the universal law of social progress. Racial evolution, national evolution, and imperial evolution are all subject to this universal social law. Nations are composed of smaller units, each an organism in itself, but united through larger organic ends in the broader unit or unity of national life. The ends of that life can never be realised by denying to the subordinate units their legitimate freedom of self-movement and self-development. A nation which seeks to do it kills itself. Empires similarly are composed of smaller organisations called nations, or popularly, states or dominions. These nations or states or dominions are themselves social organisms, larger than individuals or families or townships, but that have a specific end unto themselves, an end that is determined by the peculiarities of their special structure and environment. But they are united organically to the larger organism of the empire, and have, therefore, necessarily to seek their own specific ends and realise them only through the larger ends and the broader unity of the imperial whole. These larger imperial ends or this broader imperial unity can never be realised and perfected by denying to the subordinate national units their legitimate freedom of self-movement and self-development. An empire that seeks to do it kills itself. The cure of rampant imperialism must ultimately come through the recognition of the truth of this fundamental social principle. Modern imperialism is trading upon a mere half-truth. Its main strength comes from its pretensions to work up a larger unity of mankind than has as yet been realised. We may deny the validity of these pretensions, but we cannot refuse to accept the grandeur of its ideals.

THE NATURE OF THE EMPIRE-IDEA.

The empire-idea offers a broader ground for the unification of humanity than the nation-idea, even as the nation idea offers a broader basis of human fellowship than the unity of tribal or racial relations. This is the fundamental claim to superiority of the empire-idea. It is the claim, really, of a broader generalisation and a higher synthesis. The family, the tribe, the race, the nation, all these are what may be called social syntheses ; each succeeding synthesis being broader and higher than the preceding ones. The social synthesis offered by the empire-idea is broader and higher than all the others. The first condition, therefore, of the realisation of the true empire-idea, is a correct and clear understanding of the nature of this synthesis.

THE NATURE OF SOCIAL SYNTHESES.

Now every synthesis is the fruit of some antecedent antithesis. It is essentially of the nature of a settlement of contending claims, and a reconciliation of opposing interests. The value of a synthesis lies entirely in its capacity to work out this settlement and reconciliation. The family is a social synthesis, because it offers, through its larger and collective life, in which all the individual members of the family fully participate, a basis for the reconciliation of their divergent individual activities and interests. The failure to work out this reconciliation would inevitably break up the unity and solidarity of the family life, and thus destroy its usefulness; for the simple reason that it would then cease to be a synthesis at all. The unity of the family-life endures only so long as its collective authority and interests are not identified with those of any particular member of the family. Of course, this collective life and authority must have some concrete vehicle for itself, and must use some member of the family for this purpose. But the detachment of the head of the family from the passions and prejudices of the individual members of it, and equally the almost absolute merging of his own individual ends and interests in the general ends and interests of the family, preserves the real value of the synthesis. It was this detachment of the head of the family, and his self-effacement in the interests of the common life of the family which he represented, that helped very materially to perpetuate the joint-family system in India. And it is the loss of this detachment, leading to an inevitable decline of the moral authority of the head of the family over the individual members of it, that has been gradually bringing about the disruption of that old family system. Similarly, the tribe is a social synthesis, larger than the family, because it offers a ground of reconciliation to the rival claims and conflicting interests of different families, included in the tribal unit. And this synthesis also endures so long as the collective life and au hority of the tribe, though formally vested in particular individuals or families, yet really stands above them all, and, on account of this independence, or rather, more correctly speaking, transcendence, —it is able to harmonise in itself the conflicting interests of the different families comprising the tribe. Whenever this collective life and authority of the tribe loses this character, whenever its representative or representatives identify this life and authority with the particularities either of their own or of any other individual's or family's life and interests, the social synthesis is really broken up; even though the social authority may be exercised through mere brute force, whether actual or potential. The real value of the next higher social synthesis, namely that of the nation, also consists in the same fact,—in its power to reconcile, in its larger life and ideals, the divergent and oftentimes conflicting activities and interests of individuals, and families, and tribes, and races, who go to make up the collective life of the nation. And this synthesis also similarly endures only so long as the right and authority of the collective life of the nation, though necessarily vested in or represented by particular individuals or even special families or classes, does not identify itself with any part or particularity of the nation. Such identification really means the usurpation of the right and authority of the whole by a part of it. And such usurpation inevitably breaks up the synthesis, though here also the exercise of the usurped authority may be long continued through sheer brute force. The empire-idea is also a social synthesis, much larger and higher no doubt than the other social syntheses, but as a synthesis, it must fulfil these essential conditions. It must be a ground of reconciliation of divergent national ideals, different national geniuses, and conflicting national interests. It must mediate between different national units, and through this mediation, knit them together into a large social unity. And to do this, the Empire cannot be in any way identified with any one particular nation or particular group of nations composing it. These nations, like all other nations in the combination, shall be in the Empire, but the Empire though perpetually present in them as a high regulative idea, shall, all the same, stand perpetually above them. The Empire shall hold together the different nations composing it, by inspiring them with ideals and interests larger and higher than their isolated and smaller national ideals and interests, and by supplying them common grounds of co-operating with one another for the realisation of common ends. It shall help their evolution thiswise, but shall never permit itself to be identified with any particular nation in the imperial family. Such identification would necessarily destroy the synthesis itself, make the

Empire a party in the conflicts of national interests, and at once abrogate its right and authority to mediate between these national units and reconcile their conflicting interests.

A TERMINOLOGICAL USURPATION.

An empire is a much larger unit than a nation; and the smaller can never hold the larger. Nay more. The family, the tribe, the race, the nation, the empire, all these are distinct social categories; and one cannot, therefore, be converted into the other. None of these can by mere physical or numerical expansion develop into another. A family might multiply to a hundred members, still it would be nothing more than a family; a very large family, no doubt, but never a tribe. Similarly a tribe might contain a hundred thousand or even a million individuals, but it would still be a tribe, as much as the smallest tribe, but never a race. So with races and nations also. A nation might multiply itself to any extent, might expand its territorial possessions to any lengths, but it will still be a nation, and not an empire. Even the possession of sovereign authority over many nations would not convert a nation into an empire. When a nation assumes the name of an empire on these grounds, it only adds what may be called a terminological usurpation to its already-achieved territorial usurpations. That is all.

THE ACTUAL AND THE IDEAL EMPIRE.

The imperialism with which we are familiar in history, whether ancient or modern, has been universally of this type. The acquisition of political sovereignty over immense tracts and diverse peoples has been regarded as a sufficiently sound title to the name of empire. Even this imperialism has undoubtedly been a great factor in the evolution of human society and civilisation. It was, perhaps, the only type that could be realised in early times. Even this extension of political sovereignty helped, in those days, the unification of humanity. I would not belittle the contribution of the old and imperfect imperial idea to the progress of the race. But political imperialism has practically done its work. In any case, even if it may yet claim to be able to help the evolution of primitive races, it is an absolute anachronism in relation to advanced nationalities, having a long course of historic evolution and a distinctive type of culture and civilisation behind them. Political imperialism was needed for the unification of tribes and races into national units. The political synthesis was, perhaps, the only possible form of synthesis in those primitive times. But what the modern world wants is not a political, but a social synthesis. It wants a larger and more organic formula of association than what the old-world imperialism could offer.

The new empire-idea which is undoubtedly superior to the nation-idea, is not a political theory or ideal but essentially a social synthesis. Its superiority lies in the fact that it offers a much larger field and formula of human fellowship and human association than any other social synthesis.

The Nationalities Conference in Caxton Hall while raising its protest against the spirit of rampant imperialism failed, however, to prove the failure of that imperialism to serve its own legitimate end, namely, to further the cause of human fellowship and international co-operation in the pursuit of common humanitarian interests. It is, indeed, exceedingly doubtful whether any movement or organisation guided by the members of the dominant white races, however sincere their motives and strong their enthusiasm for humanity, can offer a real and effective criticism against this imperialism. The ultimate notion at the back of this imperialism is the superiority of the civilisation of the white races. It is a notion shared in with the imperialists by even the most cosmopolitan of the white peoples. And consequently the real appeal of the opponents of imperialism is based upon what the practical politician and the working statesman of the world dismiss as "considerations of abstract justice." The real solution of the problem, the true cure of the evils, of imperialism will come from a new philosophy of history and human society. We are moving towards that philosophy. The organic conception of society, the special contribution of the culture of the nineteenth century to the study of social phenomena, has laid the foundations of that philosophy. The truth of it is being increasingly realised in the internal movements of the dominant nations of the world. It is this conception that is gradually helping the replacement of the old individualistic social philosophy of the eighteenth and the nineteenth centuries by modern collectivism or socialism.

THE REAL SOLUTION : TRUE INTERNATIONALISM.

Society is an organic whole, the weak and the strong, the sick and the healthy, the learned and the ignorant, the rich and the poor, the virtuous and the sinful,—all are organic parts of this social whole. And in the face of this organic interdependence upon one another, it is absolutely impossible for any individual member or any class or caste of any society to realise their own special ends without a similar realisation by other individuals or classes or castes of their own ends. Individual possessions are absolutely valueless except in a community that has attained a certain amount of economic progress and stability and can maintain a certain level of wealthy living. The preservation of personal health is dependent to a very large extent upon public hygiene and the general health of the community. Intellectual, æsthetic, and even high spiritual culture,—all these demand a certain high level of intellectual and artistic and spiritual life in the community, and this organic interdependence between individual and individual, and class and class, and between individuals and classes and the society to which they belong, demands that for the collective ends of that society upon the realisation of which really depends the realisation of all particular ends of the individuals and classes of that society,—this organic interdependence demands that the members of every society must work together,—the strong imparting his strength to the weak, the rich giving out of his wealth to the poor, the learned freely communicating his learning to the ignorant, the good giving out of his own goodness to uplift the vicious and the criminal, and in thus helping each other and bearing each other's burdens, every individual member of society shall in his own interest help forward the interest of other individuals and thereby promote the realisation of the collective end of the society to which the individuals belong. This organic conception of society really supplies the basis and the philosophy of modern collectivism. And the expansion of this organic conception from the society to universal humanity will furnish a working basis for that broad internationalism which alone will be able to correct and cure the errors and evils of modern imperialism.

WANTED A CORRECTED VIEW OF HUMAN HISTORY.

But something more also will be needed, and that is a corrected view of human history and social evolution. In Europe from the time of Hegel downwards, the history of civilisation has been conceived "as a single line of progress, which, in realising the successive stages of the Absolute Idea, flows continuously from one race or nation to another, each representing a single phase of the Absolute, a single moment in the dialectic process. This punctual conception of races and epochs, and this lineal view of development, are essentially false". European sociologists have hitherto measured and adjudged different races and cultures by an abstract and arbitrary standard derived from the history of European civilisation. And they have given to non-European culture and civilisation only a subsidiary and provisional place in their sociological scheme, "as if they were either monstrous or defective forms of life, or only primitive ancestral forms, the earlier steps of the series, that have found their completion in European society and civilisation". But, as Dr. Brajendranath Seal pointed out in his Introduction to "Vaishnavism and Christianity," more than ten years ago, "with the ethnological material at our disposal, it is a gross and stupid blunder to link on Chinese, Hindu, Semitic, Greek, Roman, Gothic, Tutonic cultures, in one line of filiation, in one logical (if not chronological) series. No race or civilisation with a continuous history represents a single point or moment. In fact, even Chinese civilisation like the Chinese language, has had a development of its own; and though in all this race history the Chinese race-consciousness has subsisted, it has still been a differentiation of the homogeneous, a development of a coherent heterogeniety, out of an incoherent homogeniety. Hindu culture, too, has passed through most of the stages observed in the growth of the Hebraic-Graeco-Romano-Gothic civilisation. The same may be said of Arabic or Mahomedan culture. To conceive these statically, to reduce each living procession to a punctual moment in a single line is to miss their meaning and purpose".

Universal Humanity is not to be figured as the crest of an advancing wave, occupying but one place at any moment, and leaving all behind a dead level. Universal Humanity is immanent everywhere and at every moment,—I will not say, a circle of which the centre is everywhere and the circumference nowhere,—but at any rate, generically present in each race-consciousness, though each race may not have reflected the perfect type or pattern. From the statical point of view, Universal Humanity, though present in each race, is diversely embodied, reflected in specific modes and forms. The ideal of Humanity is not completely unfolded in any, for each race potentially contains the fulness of the ideal, but actually renders a few phases only, some expressing lower or fewer, others higher or more numerous ones. To trace the outlines of this universal ideal, we must collate and compare the fragmentary imperfect reflections, not at all in eclectic fashion, but as we seek to discover a real species or genus among individual variations and modes;—and a Congress like this fulfils a glorious mission in helping to realise the Vision of Universal Humanity, a Vision no less wondrous than the manifestation of the Uuniverse-body of the Lord in the Geeta to Arjuna's wondering gaze. The moral unity of the Human Race is fast taking the place of many of the out-worn creeds of the ancient or mediæval world, and the Vision of Universal Humanity of which we get a tantalizing glimpse beneath the protean transformations of race and cult, is only the yet unrisen sun which looms in the horizontal mists on which it has cast its image.

It is this conception of social evolution and universal history which alone, when properly worked out, and applied to the study of the different world-cultures, will be able to offer a solution of the problem which the Nationalities Conference was trying to tackle.
